Tallinn

Footprint   Clare Thomson

Contents

About the author

Tourism was the last thing on Clare Thomson's mind when she made her first trip to Tallinn, accompanying her Estonian mother back to her homeland in 1989. She was soon swept up by the revolutionary fervour of the time and spent the next two years racing through the Soviet-occupied Baltic states, researching her book about their struggle to restore independence, *The Singing Revolution* (1991), and stringing for national newspapers. Having worked as a journalist in Paris and Brussels, she now lives in London with her husband and small daughters and continues to write, while forever seeking excuses to return to Tallinn. She is also the author of *Footprint Antwerp & Ghent*.

Acknowledgements

In memory of my Glasgow-born father, who died suddenly in Tallinn in 2002, and with love and gratitude to my Tartu-born mother, whose help with this book has been invaluable. Special thanks to Matthew, Rosa and Ella-Ingrid for their patience (sort of) and to Nana Trish and Grandpa Mike. I am also indebted to Heigo Sahk and Kristi Tarand, to Ane Härmaste, Voike Kiik, Ülle Leis and Liina Siib, Tiina Laats and the Estonian Institute, Marianne and Madis Mikko, Martin Raud, my godson Johann Hendrik Salupere and parents Andrus and Vaike, and to Delia Saneberg. Heartfelt thanks also to Estonian Air, Kay Bischoff, Krista, Kuldar and Markus Samuel Ebruk, Leelo Ilbis and the Tallinn City Tourist Office, Merike Hallik, Merike Jürna, Rosanna Kelly, Tiit Kiik, Andrus Kivirähk, Anne Kurepalu, Heiki Laan, Anne Luik, Tamara Luik, Vladimir Karassev Orgussaar, Janno Pajo, Kristel Papell, Mark Piirlaid and Regio maps, the Port of Tallinn, Ilmar Raag, Juku- Kalle Raide, Helena Risthein, Kristel Saulepp and Tallinn Airport, Elo- Hanna Seljamaa, Karl Martin Sinijärv, Triin Siinisaar, Stuart Sweeney and Critical Dance, Ehtel Halliste, Konstantin Tenman, Heie Treier, Kalev Tuubel, Toomas Tuul, Piret Viires and the Estonian Writers' Union.

Tallinn, the medieval, high-tech capital of Estonia, cradle of Skype and Kaloo, owes its fortunes and seemingly endless misfortunes to its strategic location on the eastern shore of the Baltic Sea, where northern Europe and the Orient collide. The city has been moulded by a curious combination of Teutonic efficiency and Russian extravagance. Although its Old Town is often described as 'fairy-tale', there's not a hint of tweeness in the architecture: the soaring spires of the churches and the narrow, Hanseatic merchants' houses, leaning perilously into the streets and washed with watery limes, yellows and pinks, are unfussy, even austere. The Sleeping Beauty-feel comes from the forest that encircles the Old Town, softening the edges of the rugged city walls. Seagulls wheel above the rough grey limestone castle of Toompea before spiralling down past russet turrets and the cubist jumble of red-tiled roofs to the silvery Bay of Tallinn, where cruise ships sound their horns before edging out towards Stockholm, Helsinki or St Petersburg.

The turn of the tide

The Brits have a maddening habit of muddling up 'the Baltics' and 'the Balkans'. Perhaps it's because both regions have turbulent, often tragic, pasts. The Danes seized Tallinn in the 13th century, but sold the troublesome territory to the German Teutonic Order (for a shockingly small sum), before Sweden, then Russia, moved in. The Russian Revolution gave Estonians the chance to break their chains and establish the 'first republic': in the brief period of independence between the two World Wars, the standard of living exceeded that in Finland. Both Stalin and Hitler dragged their war machines through the country, which was then illegally occupied by the Russians for nearly 50 years. Free again in 1991 following the implosion of the Soviet Union, the country lost no time in modernizing itself, and was the first former Soviet republic to be invited to join the European Union.

It's some 15 years since Estonia slipped out of the communist yoke, so it's no surprise that locals find the epithet 'post-Soviet' rather tedious. In any case, Tallinners will tell you, they were never entirely Soviet. Physically, the city looked grim, but spiritually, the westernmost outpost of Uncle Joe's unholy empire had a special glow. The memory of democracy and hard-won freedom was silently passed down the generations, and, after Stalin's demise, Tallinn had a relatively liberal cultural climate.

Tabula Rasa

Estonia's second bid for freedom coincided with the revolution in information technology, a heady combination. Veterans of the never-ending waiting lists for landline telephones leapt at the chance to buy mobile phones, while the new banks didn't bother with chequebooks. The government's introduction of paper-free meetings drew attention from around the world; there was even talk of renaming the country 'E-stonia'. Estonian programmers helped develop file-sharing (Kazoo) and online telephony (Skype), and it is hardly unusual to find the following note on the door of a temporarily closed museum: "Exhibition continues on the internet."

A certain youthful arrogance accompanied this ruthless enthusiasm for wiping away the past. The first prime minister was 32 (his foreign minister just 26).

At a glance

One of the charms of compact Tallinn, a city with just under 400,000 inhabitants, is how easy it is to get about on foot. Capital of a country that is larger than often thought (comparatively, Estonia is bigger than Denmark and smaller than Ireland), it pulls in most of the tourists, a huge chunk of the foreign investment and visiting artists and performers from around the world.

Toompea (Dome Hill)
Traditionally the haunt of foreign aristocrats, nobles, politicians and administrators, the limestone plateau of Toompea sits in splendid isolation on the southwest side of the Vanalinn (Old Town), with spectacular views of the sea and the city below. The medieval network of streets was preserved despite the devastating fire of 1684, and the craggy stone walls of the old fortress give Toompea its distinctively doughty look.

All-Linn (Lower Town)
Shaped like a kidney bean, the historic All-Linn (Lower Town) lies east of Toompea and extends north from Harju street in the south along Pikk (Long) street to the port. Wedged between the wider streets is a higgledy-piggledy scrawl of cobbled lanes, many edged with pastel-coloured medieval merchants' houses. Its focal point at all hours of the day and night is Town Hall Square. The Old Town is ringed by a rough limestone city wall, dotted with 15th- and 16th-century red-tiled towers. Beyond the wall, bastions and a former moat have been transformed into lush, rambling parkland.

Dome alone

Toomkirik stands in splendid isolation at the heart of Toompea

Kesklinn

The newer districts surrounding the Old Town (comprising Toompea and All-Linn) are known rather prosaically as Kesklinn (City Centre). The southern section stretches from west of Toompea down to Liivalaia, with its shiny new office blocks, and across to the Estonia Theatre and Opera. Much of the area was bombed during the Second World War, but there are pockets of wooden housing and plenty of handsome turn-of-the-last-century and pre-war buildings, among them the elaborate bank building, where Estonia's independence was declared in 1918.

Harbour and around

The port area, north of the Old Town, is one of Tallinn's fastest-growing neighbourhoods. The engines driving its expansion are the harbour, from where hydrofoils speed north to Helsinki, and the passenger port, where cruise ships dock. Mere puiestee (Sea Avenue) leads south alongside the Old Town from Rotermanni, a former factory district, to Viru väljak (Viru Square), which is dominated by the Viru Hotel, the city's top hotel for Western tourists in Soviet days. Although it still has a gritty feel – industrial wastelands and modern buildings hastily erected in the anything-goes chaos of the early 1990s – the area is decidedly on the up, with some of the city's trendiest bars, clubs and restaurants.

Kadriorg

This leafy seaside suburb east of the city centre grew up around the mulberry-coloured baroque palace built by Peter the Great as his summer residence. The area had its heyday as a resort in the 19th century, following the creation of the Tallinn-St Petersburg-Moscow railway. One of the chief charms of the area today is the intricately carved wooden residential architecture, much of which has been painstakingly restored.

Pirita

Famous for its pine-fringed, white-sand beach, Pirita, to the northeast, is also home to a yachting complex and resort built for the 1980 Moscow Olympics. You can rent a boat on Pirita River, which joins the Bay of Tallinn here, or wander in the wooded Metsakalmistu (Forest Cemetery), where leading Estonian political and cultural figures are buried. The Television Tower, with its Galaxy restaurant, is a poignant relic of the Soviet era, worth a visit for a whiff of the past as well as the views from the observation platform.

Kalamaja and Kopli Bay

Kalamaja ('Fish house'), Tallinn's oldest suburb, lies beside the sea northwest of the Old Town. Like so many neighbourhoods of wooden houses, it fell into neglect under Soviet rule and until recently had the reputation of being poor and slummy. Now up and coming, it has a vaguely bohemian feel. Northwest is Kopli, with pockets of wooden architecture, industrial sites, some fascinating Stalinist architecture and a beach. The grimmer bits fizzle out as you approach the cliffs of the Rocca al Mare open-air museum, an assembly of reconstructed rural architecture overlooking Kopli Bay.

A tale of two suburbs: Lasnamäe and Nõmme

At opposite ends of the city from each other, these two areas offer a perfect example of the contrast between things Soviet (Lasnamäe's cheaply built, grey, prefabricated tower blocks, where everyone lives on top of each other) and things Estonian (Nõmme's pretty wooden villas, with fences and gardens providing longed-for privacy). Lasnamäe, east of Kadriorg, is bisected by the Narva highway, route one to Russia; forested Nõmme is southwest of town on the way to party central, the coastal town of Pärnu.

Around Tallinn

Heading west from Tallinn, you will find manor houses, beaches, gentle cliffs and the wild Pakri Peninsula, best reached from Paldiski – once the Soviet Union's nuclear submarine training base. East lies Lahemaa (Land of Bays), a national park with coastal villages, romantic manor houses and rich flora and fauna. The almost deserted island of Naissaar, until recently out of bounds because of unexploded mines, is just north of the city in the Bay of Tallinn.

Trip planner

If you like it (reasonably) hot, visit Tallinn between May and August; July is usually the warmest month. Just don't expect to have it all to yourself, as summer brings swarms of sightseers and cruise-ship day-trippers to the Old Town. The climate is fickle and it can rain at any time of year. The Old Town is stunningly beautiful and peaceful when it snows (possible from November to March) but daylight is in short supply at this time of year; it gets dark at 1500 in the bleak midwinter. Most museums are closed on Mondays and/or Tuesdays; worth bearing in mind when you pick up your Tallinn Card.

24 hours

On a lightning visit, there's little point in straying beyond the Old Town's maze of medieval streets. Rise early and head for Toompea before the crowds: the streets are eerily quiet, and you will have the viewing platforms to yourself, which makes the whole experience inestimably more romantic. Head down from the Danish King's Garden to Niguliste Church, then pass the tourist office on Kullassepa before starting your Lower Town exploration at its heart, Raekoja plats. Tarry a while to take in the Town Hall, then head for the handsome Hansa houses on Lai, the 'street of theatres', home to the excellent Applied Arts Museum. As you approach the daunting spire of Oleviste Church, cut left to Laboratooriumi for an up-close view of the city walls, with a line of intact towers, then make for Fat Margaret

▶ Future perfect

Estonia had more than its share of troubles in the 20th century, so it's hard to begrudge the nation its successful start to the 21st. On the economic front, strong annual growth has seen a considerable increase in local purchasing power and, therefore, prices: bad news for tourists, though GDP in 2006 was still only 46% of the EU average per inhabitant. And in all walks of life, Estonians are proving that a tiny country can compete on a global stage. A victory at the Eurovision Song Contest in 2001 helped raise the country's profile. And, to the amazement of many – especially the neighbouring Finns – Estonia snatched three gold medals at the 2006 Winter Olympics in Turin.

A further boost will come in 2011, when Estonia will have its first European Capital of Culture. Inevitably, Tallinn and Tartu are the two candidates, though the capital is the heavyweight contender. A decision is expected in 2007, with an instant investment in the winning city's infrastructure and cultural attractions.

tower and the Maritime Museum. Pikk tänav (Long street) takes you back into town, past pretty Pühavaimu Church, in time for lunch at one of the eateries on Vene, the 'street of food'. Continue down Vene for the City Museum and the Dominican Monastery, then cut through cute Katariina käik to Müürivahe, another stretch of rugged fortifications. Admire the Viru Gates before wandering north along Uus, a characterful street with a superb baroque embassy building. Step in time to the martial music blasting out of the Mine Museum, then head back towards the heart of town for dinner.

A weekend (2-4 days)

A weekend in and around the Old Town gives you time to explore the old centre at a slightly less breathless pace. On your second day, dip a toe into the 'new town', where you will find pre-war architecture and monuments to Estonia's hard-won first period of independence. If the sun is out, head straight to Pirita Beach by bus or bicycle; energetic types can row, row, row their boats down the gentle Pirita River, admiring the proud ruins of St Birgitta Convent as they rise above the trees. Still outdoors, take a walk in stately Kadriorg Park, with its simple wooden houses and Peter the Great's grand summer palace, or get a taste of Estonian peasant life at the cliffside Rocca al Mare open-air museum. A bus ride will take you to Nõmme, a near-rural suburb with pretty painted villas nestling amid the trees; or, in the opposite direction, the compellingly claustrophobic Soviet-era tower blocks of Lasnamäe, home to nearly a third of Tallinn's population. There's more communist 'nostalgia' at Paldiski, a train ride west of Tallinn, the former Soviet submarine training base and gateway to the windswept, unspoilt Pakri Peninsula. Cyclists and loners should take a ferry to Naissaar, an idyllic and sparsely populated island where some of the paths seem not to have been trodden for years.

A week or more

Although you can do all of the following on a day trip from Tallinn, you'll have more fun if you opt for an overnight stay. For nature-lovers, Lahemaa National Park (Land of Bays) has beaches, boulders, bears and beavers, with trails through the forest and around the coast. Birdwatchers should head for the Matsalu reserve, where migrant waders throng in spring and autumn, combining the twitching with a visit to the genteel resort town of Haapsalu. Pärnu is the place for party animals, although its status as the 'summer capital' owes as much to its thriving arts scene and spa treatments as to the beachside bars and nightlife. Estonia's second city, the lively university town of Tartu, was the cradle of Estonian nationalism in the 19th century, and has a far more cerebral feel than the commerce-driven capital; from here, a boat trip down the Emajõgi River takes you to Lake Peipsi, on the Estonian-Russian border.

★ **Ten of the best**

Best

1 **Lossi plats** (Castle Square) The spirits of Estonia (the pink parliament building) and Russia (Nevsky Cathedral) face off in the foreground, with soaring Pikk Hermann Tower and enchanting woodland providing a powerful backdrop, p35.

2 **Raekoda** (Town Hall) Northern Europe's only surviving Gothic town hall is a proud, rough-hewn charmer with spectacular dragon waterspouts, p48.

3 **Katariina käik** Tallinn's most enchanting alleyway, with low vaulting, wrought-iron lamps and an unusually radical tombstone, p54.

4 **Tornide väljak** (The Square of Towers) One of the city's most breathtaking vistas, with three rampart towers shrinking into the distance, p56.

5 **Pühavaimu Church** A modest but magical medieval church with an exquisite old clock and interior, p61.

6 **Oleviste Church** Once the world's tallest edifice, it still stirs the soul, with views of Toompea and the Lower Town from its needle-thin copper spire, p61.

7 **Applied Arts Museum** Glassware, textiles, jewellery and copper work, all Tallinn traditions, p63.

8 **Kadriorg Palace** Baroque splendour in leafy surrounds, built for Peter the Great and living up to his name, p75.

9 **St Birgitta's Convent** Lofty and lonesome, these skeletal seaside ruins form one of the city's most fragile silhouettes, p82.

10 **Rocca al Mare** An open-air museum of peasant dwellings, barns and windmills, set in rolling rural landscape with clifftop views over Kopli Bay, p87.

The ★ symbol is used throughout this guide to indicate recommended sights.

Contemporary Tallinn

Like all cities, Tallinn has its fair share of myths: for example, that all the women are slim, blonde and leggy, or that there is not a single handsome or sober man in town. This misconception was exploited to witty effect during the referendum campaign in 2003, with a poster depicting a Latin-looking man above the words: "230 million males live in EU countries. European males drink less and live longer than Estonian ones. Make your man a European!"

There's more in this than that campaign's creators intended. Estonia is wedged between the free-market anarchy of post-Soviet Russia and the cool, rational, civilized Scandinavian states; the great task for Tallinn is to absorb these contradictory foreign influences without being overwhelmed by them. Its liberal economic policies have pulled in plenty of investment from Sweden, Norway and Finland; and governments across Europe are casting an envious glance at the country's pioneering flat-tax system. Yet, Tallinn is, thankfully, far from being Nordicized. For one thing, socialism, a Scandinavian touchstone, is still treated with suspicion. After the collapse of communist rule, a minority got very rich very quick, and not all of them played by the rules. Then there are problems common to east and west: drug addiction, sex tourism and prostitution, the last-named addressed in Swedish director Lucas Moodyson's harrowing film *Lilja 4 Ever* (2003), partly shot in Tallinn.

When a former foreign minister declared, deadpan, that Estonia's goal was "to become just another boring Nordic country", he may have meant that the country needed time to calm down and take stock. Annoyance at any reference to the Soviet time has given way, at least in more enlightened circles, to the admission that not *everything* was awful then – or rather, that you need not be ashamed of having lived under communism. Older Tallinners can laugh about having developed one way of speaking for public places and another for trusted friends and family, a habit some find hard to shrug off.

The attitudes of travelling Easterners and visiting Westerners towards each other have also changed: gone are the mutual misconceptions so well captured in Tõnu Õnnepalu's savagely funny novel, *Border State* (1993), about an Estonian in Paris: "When they [Westerners] hear you're from Eastern Europe, they look on you with pity and speak with hollow words, as if you were a dead relative." Now we're all in the same EU boat, although, farcically, Western press coverage of Baltic issues is still handled by correspondents in Moscow and Russia finds endless excuses not to agree its border with Estonia.

Life for many Tallinners is governed by the need to work, work, work and to advance and better themselves; many have more than one job and are slaves to their mortgages. Yet they always summon the stamina to play, play, play, perhaps unsurprising given the sheer volume of tempting bars in town, and they love to dress up for a grand occasion, and to attend concerts given by one of the many Estonian conductors who've made their reputations abroad. In a city where everyone seems to know everyone else, this isn't social climbing, more a chance to catch up with old school and university friends who happen to be in the government. Theatre, too, is popular, as a place where you can escape and laugh at yourself, hence the success of Andrus Kivirähk's play, *The Estonian Funeral*, an affectionate poke at the ritualistic mania for berry-picking and jam-making, which often results in pots of the stuff mouldering away in cupboards unopened for years.

Self-righteous Western observers used to delight in asking whether the rights of the Russian-speaking community, which makes up 40% of Tallinn's population, were being respected. In newly independent Estonia, some Russian-speakers complained about the new citizenship law, which granted automatic citizenship only to those who were citizens of the pre-war republic, including emigrés; others living in Estonia had to apply for citizenship, or choose another nationality. There is a dwindling pool of as yet undecided inhabitants with 'grey passports'. Other than that, there's surprisingly little tension. Pre-independence, differences were largely ideological (Estonians feared 'Russians' would sabotage their bid for independence, while the latter feared they would lose out in the new Estonia); now they are, as one local observer put it, 'practical'. Many Tallinners over 30 do not mix with members of the other language community, but the opposite is true for the younger generation, especially on the dancefloor. Younger Estonians do not wince when they hear Russian, and younger Russian-speakers have little trouble picking up Estonian, although more could be done to guarantee quality Estonian-language tuition in Russian-language schools.

Following Estonia's accession to the European Union and NATO, investment continues to flow into the country and almost everyone is benefiting, no matter what language they speak. And tourism is booming as the number of visiting cruise ships soars and Tallinn exploits its image as a place where the medieval saunters along in perfect harmony with the modern. Where else in the world would an early-music ensemble translate Black Sabbath lyrics into Latin, taking heavy metal back to the Middle Ages and making it sound entirely new? Workaholics by day, hedonists by night, pragmatists pretty much all the time, Estonians are hell-bent on making up for the lost time of the Soviet occupation, hence the dynamism and lack of complacency that characterize this indomitable city.

Tallinn can be reached by air, sea and rail. Ülemiste airport is 4 km from the city centre, and there are two passenger ports, both within walking distance of the Old Town.

The Old Town is easily negotiable by foot. Outside the city walls, there's a reliable and inexpensive public transport network of trolley buses, trams and electric trains. The cobbled streets of the Old Town provide bone-shaking cycling; elsewhere, the lack of hills and an expanding system of cycle lanes make it a treat. You can visit other cities and the countryside independently by hiring a car or taking coaches, although you should avoid the underfunded railway system. Local travel agencies can also arrange trips.

Tallinn is safe at all times of day and night, but beware of pickpockets in touristy areas, the Balti jaam railway station and when leaving clubs and bars late at night. Tallinn is a 24-hour city, and you can easily find somewhere to eat in the centre if you arrive after 11pm, especially on weekends. The bigger hotels are open 24 hours but, wherever you're staying, it's best to give warning of a late arrival.

Getting there

Air

Estonian Air, www.estonian-air.ee, is the main carrier to Tallinn. The best fares are invariably found online. All prices given below include tax.

From the UK and Europe There are direct flights to Tallinn from London, Manchester and Dublin, as well as Amsterdam, Berlin, Brussels, Copenhagen, Frankfurt, Gothenburg, Hamburg, Helsinki, Kiev, Milan, Moscow, Oslo, Paris, Prague, Riga, Stockholm, Vilnius and Warsaw. **Estonian Air** has nine flights per week to Tallinn from London Gatwick (2 hrs 50 mins; returns from £80), departing at 0930 (Thu, Sat), 1800 (Mon-Fri, Sun) and 1930 (Sun). There are flights from Manchester (3 hrs; from £80) at 1000 on Tuesday and Saturday and from Dublin (3 hrs; from €85) at 0045 on Monday, Wednesday and Friday. **EasyJet**, www.easyjet.com, flies direct from London Stansted once a day at 0645. Prices vary, but at the time of writing, a return fare of £45 was available. Both airlines operate a point-to-point booking system, so you can fly out with one and back with the other, depending on fares and/or the convenience of the flight times. If you prefer to use another airport, you can fly to Tallinn via Helsinki, which is served by **Finnair**, www.finnair.com; or via Stockholm or Copenhagen, served by **SAS**, www.scandinavian.net. The connection via Helsinki offers splendid views of the Old Town.

   Copterline, T 358 200 18181, www.copterline.ee, runs a helicopter hop between Helsinki and Tallinn. The 18-minute trip between Tallinn's City Hall heliport and Helsinki's Hernesaari heliport starts at £89 one-way, if booked online.

From North America There are no non-stop flights from North America to Tallinn, so the best option is to fly via another western European city. The most direct options are via Stockholm or Copenhagen, served by **SAS**, T 800 221 2350 (USA telephone sales toll free), www.scandinavian.net, flying from New York and Chicago; and via Helsinki, served by **Finnair**, **T** 800 950 5000 (USA toll free), **T** 0870 241 4411 (London), www.finnair.com, flying from New York. **SAS** belongs to the Star Alliance, which also includes **Estonian Air** and **United Airlines**; **Finnair** is part of OneWorld, to which **American Airlines** has signed up.

Airport Information **Ülemiste airport**, **T** 605 8888, www.tallinn-airport.ee, is modern and extremely manageable, with one passenger terminal. In the arrivals hall, you'll find a telephone, cash point, bureau de change, post office, café, restaurant, hairdresser and beauty salon, humidor and several local travel agencies and car-hire firms. A taxi to central Tallinn costs about 100 EEK. Bus number 2 leaves from outside the departure hall and stops near the Kaubamaja department store, a short walk from the Old Town. It costs 15 EEK, one way. The duty-free shop is open only to departing passengers. WiFi (wireless internet) access is available in the transit zone.

For passengers arriving at night, the bureau de change is open and there should be several taxis waiting. And with the city's bars and clubs just minutes away, there's little incentive to hang around.

Car
From the UK you can take a car ferry from Newcastle to Gothenburg with **DFDS Seaways**, **T** 0870 533 3000, www.dfdsseaways.co.uk, starting at £19 per person one way, £62 per car. From there you can drive to Stockholm and take a car ferry to Tallinn. You will have no trouble obtaining car insurance to drive in Estonia. A car is useful for travelling around the country, but more trouble than it's worth if you are staying in the Old Town, given the lack of parking spaces and the relative expense of paid parking. Non-residents can no longer drive into the heart of the Old Town – neither, be warned, can taxis.

Coach

Given the poor state of Estonian railways, it is much more efficient to travel to Tallinn from neighbouring countries by bus; it's also the best option for domestic journeys to Haapsalu, Pärnu and Tartu. There are buses from Riga to Tallinn (5 hrs, 4 departures per day), Vilnius (10 hrs, 2 departures per day) and St Petersburg (8 hrs, 5 departures per day). Buses arrive at the Tallinn Bus Station (Tallinna Bussiterminal/Autobussijaam), Lastekodu 46 (trams 2 or 4), **T** 681 3471, which offers money exchange and a left-luggage facility. Estonian, Russian and Finnish, but only a little English, are spoken at the bus station. A taxi to the Old Town costs 50 EEK. Trams 2 and 4 go to the Viru Hotel and buses 17a, 23 and 23a go to Vabaduse väljak. Coaches also arrive and depart from the port. Expect delays if crossing the Russian border by road at peak times, for example on Fridays. State-run coaches have priority. The situation has improved since Estonia joined the EU.

Eurolines, **T** 06800 909, www.eurolines.com, runs services to Tallinn from many cities, including Kaliningrad, Moscow, Kiev, Stuttgart, Munich, Cologne, Riga, Vilnius and St Petersburg. From London there is a service to Tallinn via Riga and Vilnius (3 days, £226, 4 departures per week).

Ferry

From Europe Tallinn is easily reached from Stockholm or Helsinki. **Tallink**, **T** 640 9808, www.tallink.ee, has daily ferries from Stockholm, departing early evening and arriving the following morning, from 350 EEK one way, plus 850 EEK for a car; cabins for two start at 1450 EEK.

Several companies run ferries year-round from Helsinki, a 3½-hour crossing, including **Tallink**, **Eckerö Line**, **T** 631 8606, www.eckero line.fi/en, and **Viking Line**, **T** 666 3966, www.vikingline.fi. Expect to

! In the 16th century it was so cold that you could walk across the frozen sea between Estonia and Sweden.

pay from €17 per person and €17 for a car, both one way. From late spring until late autumn, depending on the weather, catamarans (which also take cars) cut the journey time to 90 minutes. **Nordic Jet Line**, T 613 7000, www.njl.info, runs catamarans, as do **Silja Line**, T 611 6661, www.silja.com/english, and **Tallink**. Expect to pay from €30 one way or €85 for a car and two passengers. **Silja Line** also sails to Rostock and St Petersburg; the 12-hr trip to the latter costs from €36 return (lounge seat), €92 return (two-person cabin).

Ferries and catamarans arrive at the Passenger Port (Reisisadam), T 631 8550, www.ts.ee, 500 m north of the Old Town, which has a money exchange, a telephone, a café, a duty-free shop, a left-luggage facility and ATMs. A taxi to the centre costs 50 EEK. There are four terminals, A-D, so check where your return boat leaves from.

The fastest way to reach Tallinn from Helsinki is with **Lindaline**, T 699 9333, www.lindaliini.ee, whose hydrofoil services (summer only) cut the crossing time to 1½ hours. A return costs about €35. Lindaline uses the Linnahall Speedboat Harbour, which is about five minutes' walk from the Old Town. Trams 1 and 2 go from Viru väljak to the Linnahall stop.

Several harbours welcome private boats. For details, check the website of the **Estonian Marine Tourism Association**, www.agentuur.ee/sadamad, or the **Border Guard**, www.pv.ee.

Train

There are international links to St Petersburg (9 hrs) and Moscow (14 hrs) from the main railway station, Balti jaam, Toompuiestee 35, T 615 6850, www.evrekspress.ee, just behind Toompea. It has a left-luggage facility, bistro, casino, showers and an ATM, although this often runs out of money. From Balti jaam, you can walk or take a taxi into the Old Town; trams 1, 2 and 5 go to Viru väljak.

! Look out for these common abbreviations: *puiestee* (avenue) to pst; *maantee* (boulevard) to mnt; and *tänav* (street) to tn. These are always used locally.

Getting around

Bus

The city bus terminal is on Viru väljak; pick up a public transport map, **Tallinn Ühistranspordi Kaart**, made by Regio and available from the Tourist Office, bookshops and kiosks. Tickets for taxi buses, which depart from Kaubamaja street, the Estonia Theatre and the Merekeskus shopping centre near the port, cost 12 EEK and you pay the driver when you board. Further information is available at www.veeb.tallinn.ee/transport and www.tallinn.ee. Buses for destinations outside Tallinn leave from both the Balti jaam (for destinations near Tallinn) and Tallinn Bus Station (Autobussijaam).

For bus schedules around Estonia, consult www.bussireisid.ee. Buses for **Haapsalu**, **Pärnu** and **Tartu** leave from the main bus terminal, Lastekodu 46, **T** 680 0900. Book in advance if possible. Buses for **Tartu** leave every half-hour and the journey takes 2½-3 hours, 50-75 EEK; to **Pärnu** buses leave hourly, taking two hours, 50-70 EEK. Buses for **Haapsalu** leave hourly, taking just under two hours, 45-65 EEK. For **Matsalu Nature Reserve**, there are six buses daily to Lihula, 40-68 EEK, 3 km from the visitor centre.

Car

A car is only really useful if you are staying some distance out of the Old Town. Driving used to be surprisingly aggressive but is getting better, although reckless overtaking on the faster roads is still common. Estonians almost never hoot. The quality of the roads out of Tallinn is uneven and the name 'motorway' may strike you as inappropriate for many of the country's two-lane highways. There is no shortage of petrol stations and petrol costs around the third of the price in the UK. The speed limit is 50 kph in town, 90 kph out of town and 110 kph on some bigger roads out of town in summer. Limits change frequently, so pay attention to the signs. Front and back seatbelts are compulsory, headlights must be on at all times

Travel extras

Climate People think of Tallinn as cool, even in summer, but, to the surprise of many residents, temperatures during the past few summers have reached the mid-30s in July, while 2003 was the hottest summer on record. Light sleepers may find it hard to kip during the white nights, when it hardly gets dark at all for about a week at midsummer. The tourist season lasts from late April to early October, peaking in June and July, when the Old Town is packed with cruise-ship day-trippers. Although daylight is in short supply in winter – it gets dark at 3pm in December – Tallinn is uncrowded and stunningly beautiful in the snow, which is falling at increasingly bizarre times of year, as early as October and as late as April. The coldest month is February, when temperatures can sink to about -10°C and even, occasionally, as low as -40°C.

Health Estonia's health service is up to EU standards, but much cheaper. Take out health insurance before travelling. When venturing into rural areas, particularly Lahemaa park and around Lake Peipsi, be warned that ticks can carry encephalitis, so vaccination is advised. Have your shots at least two weeks before possible exposure.

Money The Estonian currency is the Estonian kroon (EEK). As long as you have a compatible credit/debit card and sufficient funds, using an ATM is the most convenient way of keeping in pocket. Tallinn is a relatively cheap city: the minimum daily budget for food and accommodation only is €20, and you can live extremely comfortably on €70 a day.

Visas Citizens of all EU countries, Iceland, Latvia, Lithuania, Norway and Switzerland, USA, Australia and New Zealand are exempt from visa requirements for up to 90 days. Canadian citizens need visas. Some citizens can enter Estonia with Latvian or Lithuanian visas. For visa information, consult www.vm.ee.

and there is zero tolerance for drinking when driving. You must have snow tyres (available from many of the petrol stations) in winter, and look out for moose, especially in July. For road information, visit www.tourism.tallinn.ee.

Cycling

Old Tallinn is not suited to cycling, as it is hilly and cobbly. It is easier outside the Old Town, but do watch out for car drivers, who are not always cycle-friendly, especially at crossroads. The growing network of cycling lanes further out, for example towards Kadriorg, Pirita, Viimsi and Rocca al Mare, offers the safest and most pleasant cycling in town. The best times for cycling around Tallinn in summer are between 2000 and 0730. Cycling is an ideal way to visit rural areas, as well as the islands of Naissaar, Kihnu and Vormsi. Regio and EO-map publish good cycling maps (see pxxx), available in bookshops.

Public transport

There is no underground in Tallinn. However, an efficient and inexpensive network of **buses**, **trolleybuses**, **trams** and **taxi buses** runs from 0600 to 2300 (taxi buses run until 0100, midnight on Sundays). A ticket bought from a kiosk/newsstand costs 10 EEK (or 70 EEK for 10), while tickets bought on-board cost 15 EEK. Tickets are valid for one ride from when you punch them in an on-board machine. Season tickets cost 190 EEK for 30 days and 460 EEK for 90 days, and can be bought from kiosks.

Taxi

Taxis in Tallinn are very efficient and much cheaper than in most Western cities. You do not pay more when ordering a cab by telephone and the taxi usually arrives within 10 minutes. Taxis should have meters and must have the company logo or name of the taxi driver clearly displayed. Sadly, some taxi drivers have adopted a Prague-style approach to dealing with tourists: always check that the meter works and that the fare displayed matches

▶ Tallinn Card

Promoted as your 'Key to the Medieval Capital', the **Tallinn Card** offers substantial savings, with free entry to museums and unlimited public transport, discounts in shops and restaurants and a city map, it's particularly useful if you're staying outside the Old Town, or if you're planning to visit the districts beyond it.

The most basic card, which costs 130 EEK, lasts for six hours; the 24-hour card costs 350 EEK, the 48-hour one 400 EEK and the 72-hour version 450 EEK. All, bar the six-hour one, include an official sightseeing tour, worth 200 EEK on its own, and an assortment of freebies ranging from bowling to free entry to the Hollywood nightclub. You can pick up the card from the tourist offices at Kullassepa 24/Niguliste 2, the port, the Estravel stand at the airport, the train station and several city-centre hotels. A guidebook, included as part of the package, explains exactly what you're getting for your money; you can also find details at www.tallinn.ee/tallinncard.

Many museums are closed on Monday and/or Tuesday, so it's best to check the opening hours before you buy the Tallinn Card, in particular the six-hour version.

For children under 14, the cards are half price.

the published fare (on the back-seat door or in front of the passenger seat). You should also ask for an approximate price, using Estonian if possible: "Kui palju?" (How much?). It doesn't matter if you can't understand the answer; you'll have established that you're on the ball. As a rough guide, if you're quoted more than 150 EEK to get from the airport to the Old Town, move swiftly on. There are taxi ranks at the airport, train and bus stations, at Club Hollywood, the Domina City, Viru and Olümpia hotels, and at major shopping centres. You can also try hailing a taxi in the street, **Tulika**, **T** 1200. The minimum fare is 35 EEK and the price per kilometre is about 7 EEK. **Bicycle Taxis**, **T** 508 8810, www.velotakso.ee, offers environmentally friendly one-hour guided tours for 300 EEK.

Walking
It is easy to get around on foot, although sensible footwear is best on the bumpy cobbles of the Old Town, as well as in the Vabaduse väljak and Harbour areas. A gentle stroll around Toompea and the Lower Town takes around four hours maximum. It takes about 20 minutes to walk from Raekoja plats to Liivalaia in the south, to the port in the north, or to Kalamaja; Kadriorg is 40 minutes' walk away. Other areas are best reached by public transport.

Tours

Numerous local tour operators have sprung up in Estonia over the past few years, from tiny agencies to full-blown travel companies. Some offer fixed itineraries and most will organize tailor-made trips.

Boat tours
You can charter a boat with captain for trips in the Bay of Tallinn and to islands near the capital from Pirita Harbour; contact Valdek Kallas, **T** 521 0159. **Bona Reisid**, Estonia puiestee 1/3, **T** 630 6670, www.bonareisid.ee, offers excursions in Tallinn and to Lahemaa National Park and the islands of Kihnu, Naisaar, Vormsi and Prangli, as well as themed tours of manor houses. Tailor-made tours can be arranged. For holiday trips, including accommodation and guides, plus sea transport to Kihnu, contact **Kihnurand Travel Agency**, Kihnu vald, Pärnumaa, **T** 446 9924, www.kihnu.ee/kihnurand. Underwater trips exploring some of Estonia's 40,000 shipwrecks are available with **Maremark**, L Koidula 38, **T** 601 3446, www.maremark.ee. Diving courses, trips and equipment hire are available.

Bus tours

Reisiexpert, Roosikrantsi 19, **T** 610 8616, www.travel2baltics.com, offers the 'Tallinn City Official Tour', a 2½-hour overview of Tallinn. Buses depart three times daily, April to October, from the *Viru*, *Radisson* and *Olümpia* hotels and from terminals A and D at the passenger port. From late-October to March there are two tours daily. Tickets cost 200 EEK, children 100 EEK, and are available from hotels, ferries, buses and the Port of Tallinn Tourist Information Centre (terminal A).

Cycle tours

City Bike OÜ, Tallinn City Camping, Pirita tee (near the Song Bowl), **T** 511 1819, www.citybike.ee, takes groups or individuals on guided evening tours of Pirita beach, the inland forest and meadows, the Old Town and the harbour. Leaving from Pirita tee, it's an easy-paced two-hour circuit. Tours depart at 1100 and 1700 daily and cost 220 EEK, including vest, helmet and water; book at least an hour in advance. City Bike also organizes cycling tours to Lahemaa and Paldiski.

Helicopter tours

Kareliacopters, Aianduse tee 71, Tallinn, **T** 504 4122, www.kareliacopters.ee, offers island-hopping trips to Prangli, Aegna and Naisaar, and to the country's more remote islands.

Hiking trails

RMK, Viljandi maantee, **T** 628 1500, www.rmk.ee/eng, manages hiking trails and has accommodation in forest bungalows and campsites, as well as on the coast and islands. The **Estonian Ramblers Association**, Raekoja plats 18, **T** 515 9881 www.matk.ee/english, details paths in Kuusalu, Paldiski and Naisaar on its website.

Walking tours

The city is awash with multilingual guides (former teacher Kristi Tarand, kristi@eam.ee, is among the most entertaining). If you have a theme in mind, book in advance with the Tourist Office. **Medieval Tours**, Kotzebue 7-15, T 641 4338, www.hot.ee/medieval, offers tours through the Old Town, with festive meals and actors and musicians bringing the past to life (minimum 10 people). If you'd prefer to set your own pace, the **Old Town Audioguide** is available from the Tourist Office for 225 EEK.

Tourist information

The main **Tourist Information Centre** is just around the corner from Raekoja plats at Kullassepa 4, Niguliste 2, **T** 645 7777, www.tourism.tallinn.ee. *Sep Mon-Fri 0900-1800, Sat and Sun 1000-1700; Oct-Apr Mon-Fri 0900-1900, Sat and Sun 1000-1700; Jul-Aug Mon-Fri 0900-2000, Sat and Sun 1000-1800.* It can put you in touch with specialist guides and provide free city maps and information about accommodation, restaurants, sights and what's on. It also sells postcards, souvenirs, the Tallinn Card and brochures about various aspects or areas of the town (for 25 EEK). It's also worth checking out the official tourism website, www.tourism.tallinn.ee. Staff can suggest guides if you have a particular interest (but these must be booked in advance) and can provide information about accommodation, restaurants and entertainment.

There is another information centre, **Tallinn Port Tourist Information Office**, at the port at Terminal A, Sadama 25, **T** 631 8321, www.portoftallinn.ee. *Daily 0800-1630, except public holidays.* It has information on ferry, bus and train schedules as well as local travel agencies.

! At the time of writing, UK£1 = 23 Estonian kroons (EEK); €1 = 15.6 EEK; US$1 = 12 EEK.

Outside Tallinn

Haapsalu, Posti 37, **T** 473 3248, www.haapsalu.ee. *15 May-15 Sep Mon-Fri 0900-1800, Sat and Sun 1000-1500, 16 Sep-May Mon-Fri 0900-1700.*

Lahemaa, c/o Lahemaa Visitor Centre, Palmse Manor, Palmse, **T** 95555, info@lahemaa.ee. *May-Aug daily 0900-1900, Sep daily 0900-1700, Oct-Apr Mon-Fri 0900-1700.*

Pärnu, Rüütli tänav 16, **T** 447 3000, www.parnu.ee. *Summer Mon-Fri 0900-1800, Sat 0900-1600, Sun 1000-1500.Winter Mon-Fri 0900-1700. Free booklet discovering Pärnu.*

Tartu, Raekoja plats 14, **T/F** 744 2111, www.visittartu.com. *Mon-Fri 0900-1700, Sat 1000-1500.*

Maps

Maps by **Regio**, www.regio.ee, and **EO Map**, www.eomap.ee, are highly recommended; the tourist office also gives out a free one-page map of Tallinn's Old Town and Kesklinn. It also hands out a free walking map of the city and the local listings booklet *Tallinn This Week*, published fortnightly.

Useful websites

www.tallinn.ee Official site for the city of Tallinn.
www.tourism.tallinn.ee Official tourism guide to the city.
www.tallinn.info A virtual guide to the capital.
www.visitestonia.com Official tourism site for Estonia.
www.art.ee and **www.kunstikeskus.ee** Art.
www.welcometoestonia.com Useful for trip-planning.
www.einst.ee History, culture and society.
www.wifi.ee WiFi hotspots in Estonia.
www.estonica.org Online encyclopaedia.
www.ee.ww Estonian wide-web, in English too.
www.kulture.info Cultural events calendar.
www.ibs.ee/dict Estonian-English dictionary.
www.mois.ee Manor houses in Estonia.

Tallinn

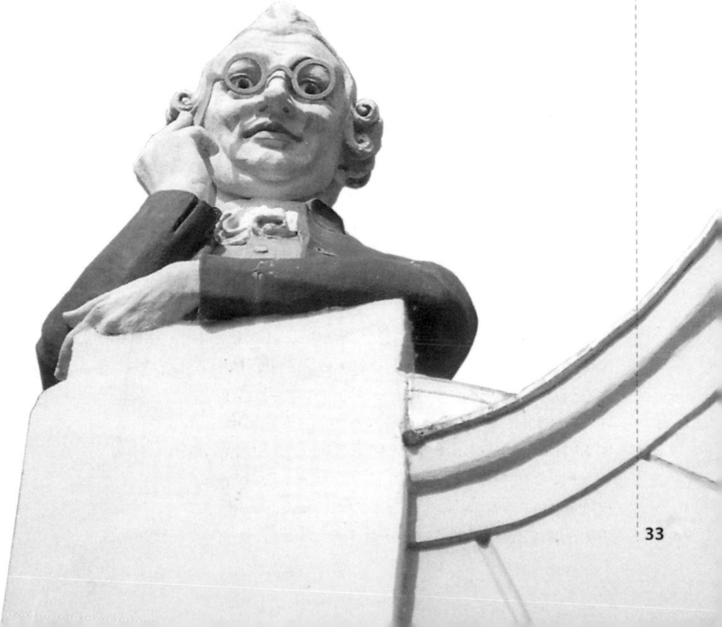

Toompea 35
The seat of power for more than a millennium, with stunning views to match.

All-Linn 46
The city's Hanseatic and hedonistic heart.

Kesklinn 65
Monuments to the trials and triumphs of the 20th century, plus the glitzy skyscrapers of the 21st.

Harbour and around 71
Renovated warehouses, blowsy booze shops and some of the coolest bars and clubs in town.

Kadriorg 74
Peter the Great's stately summer playground.

Pirita 78
The city's seaside resort, fringed by forest.

Kalamaja and Kopli Bay 84
Shabby but increasingly chic seafront stretch.

Lasnamäe 88
One third of Tallinners can't be wrong.

Nõmme 90
Swathes of forest and the spirit of the 1930s.

Toompea

Toompea is spooky, windswept, remote and aloof, and Estonians are understandably ambiguous about it. Although an Estonian stronghold was established here in the 11th century, Dome Hill (as the name translates) was the seat of foreign power and nobility between the 13th century and Estonia's declaration of independence in 1918. Tension between the noble Upper Town and the Lower Town, home to merchants and craftsmen, often ran high, hence the wall and gatehouses that separate the two. Today, the intricate streets are medieval in layout, but many of the buildings were built after the Great Fire of 1684 and are neoclassical in appearance. The most imposing building is the meringue-like Alexander Nevsky Cathedral, completed in 1900 and erected as an unmistakable symbol of Russian authority. Much older is the Toomkirik (St Mary's Cathedral), an austere and awesomely dignified structure around which leaves whirl in windy weather. The hated hammer and sickle flew from Toompea castle's tallest tower, Pikk Hermann, from 1944 until it was boldly replaced by the Estonian tricolour in 1989. Today, Toompea is still the seat of power, with an abundance of elegant government buildings and embassies, while the glorious houses have been snapped up by diplomats and a handful of wealthy locals.

▸▸ *See Sleeping p125, Eating and drinking p143*

◉ Sights

★ Lossi plats (Castle Square)
T 631 6357. *Tours Mon-Fri 1000-1600; book in advance.*
Map 2, J1, p253

Toompea's main square has been the site of a fortress since ancient times. The Teutonic castle was built by the German Knights of the Sword in 1229 and improved by their successors, the

Tallinn is like a discharged conscript who is
desperate to make up for lost time.
He works hard and he plays hard.
He can't wait to cast off that ugly uniform,
slip into an ultra-modern suit
and let his hair grow long again.
Yet he feels a little nostalgic about those army
days, because the knowledge then gained
may serve him all his days.

*Andrus Kivirähk, playwright, novelist, journalist
and leading commentator in Tallinn, 2003.*

Livonian Order. All that remains today, however, are the west and south walls and three grey towers. The dizzyingly high Pikk Hermann (Tall Hermann) was completed in the late 15th century.

State Assembly/Parliament

Lossi plats 1a, **T** 631 6357, www.riigikogu.ee. *Tours Wed-Fri 1000-1600; book in advance. Free. Map 2, J1, p253*

Rational and elegant, the pink-and-white neoclassical parliament building, rebuilt after a fire in 1918, provides a fine antidote to the florid flamboyance of Nevsky Cathedral. Inside, however, there's a surprise: the hall has been renovated to the style of the first Republic and is pure Expressionism, with lemon ceilings, ultramarine walls and a dizzying zigzag motif.

Alexander Nevsky Cathedral

Lossi plats 10, **T** 644 3484. *Daily 0800-1900. Free. Map 2, J2, p253*

Estonians loathe this neo-Byzantine symbol of Tsar Alexander III's Russification policy, named after the Russian noble who defeated Christian crusaders in 1242, and sigh with resignation when this rippling, fudge-coloured symbol of foreign rule is used to illustrate yet another travel article. Some locals, however, concede that it is an impressive piece of architecture and that the richly decorated interior, awash with icons and mosaics, is worth at least a glimpse.

Some say Nevsky is cursed because it is built on the grave of Kalev, Estonia's ancient mythical king and father of Kalevipoeg, the eponymous hero of Estonia's national epic. Created in the 19th century to cement a sense of national identity, Kalevipoeg celebrates Estonian values, such as hard work and perseverance. The hero, who is constantly having to fend off invaders, winds up trapped in hell, but we are assured that he will rise again to build a new Estonia.

The new orthodoxy

Once a symbol of Russian oppression, the Tsarist-era Nevsky Cathedral is now acquiring iconic status as the city's most popular touristic image.

Toomkirik (St Mary's Cathedral)

Toom-Kooli 6, **T** 644 4140, www.eelk.ee/tallinna.toom. *Services in Estonian (Sun at 1000) and Latvian (3rd Sun of the month at 1300); organ concerts Sat at 1200.*   *Map 2, H2, p253*

Built by the Danes in the first half of the 13th century, St Mary's looks much as it did in the 15th century, although the wonderfully sparse interior was rebuilt after the 1684 fire. The white walls, with red and white trimmings around the pointed windows, look as if they are alive with giant crustaceans: in fact, these are the coats-of-arms of noble families, and many date from the early 17th century.

One of the most elaborate tombstones in the church is that of the French-born general **Pontus de la Gardie**, sculpted by Arendt Passer in 1595. De la Gardie was an impoverished but skilled noble warrior who was high commander for the Swedes during the Livonian War. His descendants were influential figures, at one time owning Haapsalu and the island of Saaremaa. De la Gardie had the good fortune to marry into a noble Swedish family, but the ill fortune to drown in the Narva River in 1585, four years after recapturing Narva from the Russians.

The importance of the Scottish-born admiral Samuel Greig (1735-1788), who served in the Tsarist army and was a favourite of Catherine II, is illustrated by a splendid white marble monument, sculpted by Giacomo Quarenghi, architect of the Narva Gate in St Petersburg. The obelisk monument recalls **Ferdinand Von Tiesenhausen**, a scion of one of Estonia's most prestigious Baltic German families, and son-in-law of Russia's General Kutuzov (of Battle of Borodin fame). Von Tiesenhausen died at the Battle of Austerlitz in 1805 and his corpse was brought to Tallinn by his brother and finally laid to rest in St Mary's; he was reputedly the inspiration for Tolstoy's Duke Bolkonsky in *War and Peace*.

● *North of the cathedral, climb up the Patkuli Stairs to a platform for a bird's-eye view of Toompea.*

▶ Skin trade

At midnight, as the lid of Pontus de la Gardie's tomb in St Mary's Cathedral begins to quiver, out crawls the wretched general. Wearily, he clambers onto his horse and trots round town selling skins – human skins. When de la Gardie won Narva back from the Russians in 1581, he massacred 7000 locals in revenge for the brutal killing of 4000 people by Russian forces when they seized the Estonian town of Paide eight years earlier. According to legend, the French commander will rest in peace only when he has rid himself of the skins of those he killed. Centuries on, he is still peddling his sinister wares.

Stenbock House
Rahukohtu 3. *Map 2, G2, p253*

On your left, before you reach the Patkuli Stairs, is a vast white, neoclassical 18th-century structure, built in the 19th century to link the Upper Town to the railway. It is now home to the Estonian cabinet and its 'e-government' system, a world first, allows ministers to conduct paper-free meetings.

Noblemen's residences
Along Kohtu St. *Map 2, I-H3-4, p253*

The neoclassical building at **number 8** was designed by Carl Ludwig Engel, city architect of Tallinn. The 19th-century city palace of Count von Ungern-Sternberg (**number 6**) was built by Baltic German Martin Philip Gropius, great-uncle of architect Walter Gropius. The imposing residence of the Üexküll family (**number 4**) is once again the Finnish embassy, the purpose it served in pre-war Estonia. **Number 2** belonged to the von Tiesenhausen family.

Haunted House
Toom-Kooli 13. *Map 2, H1, p253*

Number 13 Toom-Kooli belonged to the Baltic German Taube
family, which sold it to the state after Estonia declared its
independence. During the Independence War, several British
officers were housed in Tallinn, one in this house. The unfortunate
soldier allegedly complained about the presence of ghosts and
was left so disturbed by his stay that he had to be hospitalized.
His counterparts in the Estonian army were also driven out by
spooks. Hoping to force the Taube family to buy back their
haunted property, the Estonian state took the matter to court.
It lost, as Estonian law makes no provision for the paranormal.

Kohtu street viewing platform
Map 2, G4, p253

You'll have to elbow your way through the crowds in peak season,
but it's worth it for the stunning view of Tallinn's higgledy-
piggledy rooftops, Oleviste church and the sea beyond. To the
right, you can see Pirita, Kadriorg and Lasnamäe.

Monument to the restoration of independence
Corner of Falgi tee. *Map 2, K2, p253*

At the corner of Falgi tee, a large boulder inscribed '20 August,
1991' commemorates the restoration of independence, after fears
that Soviet troops would storm Toompea had finally subsided.
The boulders were used to block the surrounding streets. On
23 August, 1989, the human chain from Tallinn to Vilnius, which
graced TV sets around the world, started on this hill. About two
million people held hands across some 600 km to commemorate
the 50th anniversary of the Molotov-Ribbentrop pact.
Neighbouring **Lindamägi** (**Linda's Hill**) is named after the

Best defence
Tallinn's formidable city walls, studded with towers, are among the best preserved in Europe.

unveiling of Adamson's graceful sculpture of Linda mourning Kalev (1920). During the Soviet time, when laying flowers here could earn you a prison sentence, it became a symbol of collective grief for victims of Soviet oppression. A plaque reads simply: "To remember those taken away." Just south lies the peaceful **Hirvepark** (**Deer Park**).

Kiek in de Kök
Komandandi 2, **T** 644 6686. *Tue-Sun 1030-1800. 25 EEK, 8 EEK concessions, family ticket 30 EEK. Preschool children free. Free every last Fri of the month or with Tallinn Card. Map 2, K3, p253*

The city's strongest tower ('Peep in the Kitchen' in Low German) earned its nickname because those guarding it claimed they could watch what was happening in the kitchens of the houses below. It certainly stood the heat in the Livonian War, playing a vital role in the defence of Tallinn against the Russians. The prolonged siege of 1577 so frustrated the attackers that they blasted a huge hole in the tower, but it stood proud and the city held out. Inside is a museum devoted to Tallinn's fortifications and military history, with temporary photography exhibitions on the lower floors. "Don't pull, please," warns an intriguing sign on one cannon.

Danish King's Garden
Map 2, J2, p253

From Kiek in de Kök, you can stroll through the park to the **Danish King's Garden**, supposedly the site of a key episode in Denmark's history. King Waldemar II, who conquered Tallinn in the early 13th century, apparently pitched his tent here during the brutal battle for control of the city. Hard pressed by the resilient Estonians, he prayed that God would grant him victory, whereupon a red flag with a white cross fell from the sky. This miraculous visitation rallied his troops enough to carry the day, and the *Dannebrog* was adopted as the

Heads, shoulders, knees and toes
Kalevipoeg, Estonia's mythical hero, is left trapped in hell at the end of the epic that bears his name. You need only linger in Tallinn's Šnelli Park.

Danish national flag. Neighbouring **Megede (Maiden Tower)** now houses the Neitsitorn café (see p145). The tower dates back to the 14th century, and was enlarged the following century.

Lühike jalg (Short Leg)
Map 2, I3, p253

The streets connecting the Upper and Lower Towns were fortified in the middle of the 15th century, creating the 'Wall of Hatred'. The two original gates at the top of Lühike jalg were closed at night to prevent circulation between the two sections of the divided city.

Adamson-Eric Museum

Lühike jalg 3, **T** 644 5838, www.ekm.ee/adamson-eric. *Wed-Sun 1100-1800, closed Mon-Tue. 15 EEK, children and students 5 EEK. Free with Tallinn Card.   Map 2, I3, p253*

This 16th-century building houses a permanent collection of works by one of Estonia's most impressive and eclectic artists, Adamson-Eric (1902-1968). A painter, portraitist and applied artist, he studied in Paris and Berlin, where he drew inspiration from Cubism, Fauvism and the Bauhaus. His ceramics are mouth-watering.

All-Linn (Lower Town)

Tallinn's Lower Town is the best-preserved medieval walled city in northern Europe. Ironically, this is partly because it was long considered a provincial outpost by the many foreign powers that ruled it, a place not even, in the end, worth maintaining as a fortress town. If Toompea is the seat of power, this is the soul of the city.

The Lower Town, a delectable jumble of cobbled streets and sharply angled terracotta rooftops, has an austere northern look, thanks to the locally quarried limestone with which so many of the buildings were constructed. Neglected under Soviet rule, the narrow, triangular-topped Gothic merchants' houses and the unusually sober baroque buildings have largely been renovated and freshened up. The main arteries are Lai (Wide) street, the 'street of theatres', Pikk (Long) street, the 'street of guilds', and Vene (Russian) street, named after the Russian merchants who settled in this eastern neighbourhood centuries ago.

The Lower Town is Tallinn for many visitors, for its array of bars, cafés, restaurants and shops as well as for its looks, but it's still unspoilt and dreamily romantic. You will pay more for a beer on Raekoja plats than anywhere else, but the view of the square, whether in winter snow or under a blue summer sky, is unforgettable.

▸▸ *See Sleeping p127, Eating and drinking p145, Bars and clubs p165*

Panicke attack

Two stones forming an L-shape near Raeapteek (obscured by café terraces in summer) are all that remains of a cross marking the unusual fate of a religious man. In 1695 an irascible, inebriated priest called Panicke was so outraged by the poor quality of a meal at a local inn that he killed the waitress who had served him with an axe. The contrite cleric confessed to the crime and asked to be executed on the spot. How the citizens of Soviet Tallinn, where the customer was never right, must have longed to follow his example.

 Sights

Raekoja plats (Town Hall Square)
Map 2, H5, p253

Tallinn's Town Hall Square has an enchanting elegance that's maddeningly hard to pin down. Apart from the town hall, which looks pretty much as it did in the 15th century, most of the pastel-tinted buildings went up in the 19th and 20th centuries and, taken individually, they are far from masterpieces. Together, though, they make for one of Europe's most appealing squares, especially on a summer evening, when the shade of the sky seems tailor-made for the gentle pinks, whites and blues of the façades.

Previously a market place and trading centre, the square has witnessed festivals and fairs as well as floggings and executions. Flooded with cafés in summer, it is the beating heart of the Lower Town, bustling with traders, artisans and merry-makers, and is the backdrop for the medieval Old Town Days festival, the Christmas market and the hailing of national heroes, be they Olympic champions or Eurovision winners.

★ Raekoda (Town Hall)

Raekoja plats 1, **T** 645 7900. *Jul-Aug Mon-Sat 1000-1600, 35 EEK. Tower May-Aug 1100-1800, 25 EEK. Exhibition Hall Tue-Sat 1200-1600, 10 EEK. Free with Tallinn Card. Map 2, H5, p253*

Recently scrubbed clean to reveal the original yellow colour of the limestone – much to the surprise of the locals, who'd grown up with it being grey – the Town Hall has been a centre for administration and entertainment since at least 1322, although its present incarnation, with an elegant arcade, dates back to 1404 and the spire is baroque. Highlights inside include the coloured columns of the Citizens' Hall, the elaborate carvings on the magistrates' bench and the views from the tower – well worth the slightly perilous ascent. During the Christmas period, there is a market in the cellar selling handicrafts, local produce and cakes.

Raeapteek (Town Hall Chemist)

Raekoja plats 11, **T** 631 4860, raeapt@hot.ee. *Mon-Fri 0900-1900, Sat 0900-1700, Sun 0900-1600. Map 2, G6, p253*

A pharmacy has stood here since at least 1422 and still functions today, making it one of the world's oldest. Centuries ago, drugs were made using anything from ground horn to swallows' nests and burnt hedgehogs; today, perhaps disappointingly, the products on sale are the same as you'd find in your average high-street pharmacy. Such was the fame of the Burchart family, who ran it for generations, that Peter the Great supposedly called for Johann Burchart VI to attend to him on his deathbed. (He did not arrive on time.)

The names of the streets around Raekoja plats, such as Voorimehe (Coachmen), Vana Turu Kael (Old Market Neck) and Kullassepa (Goldsmith), convey something of the bustle of by gone days. Most of the streets had several names, one each for the Estonian, German and Russian communities, but these were standardized in the 19th century.

▶ **Local hero**

At the top of the Town Hall's spire is the Vana Toomas (Old Thomas) weather vane, named after a poor local lad who rose to fame during a parrot-shooting contest. The competition was open only to the rich, but none hit the target; young Thomas, however, felled the bird with one twang of his simple wooden bow. The toffs took umbrage at his temerity, but the Great Guild's alderman took the lad under his wing and trained him to be a town guard, a task he performed with diligence and daring into old age. Estonians love people who get the best of their supposed betters, and the tale of Thomas inspired the knickerbocker-clad figure on the weather vane, an unofficial symbol of the city. First put up in 1530 (the current figure is a replica), Old Thomas has watched over Raekoja plats ever since.

Town Prison Museum of Photography

Raekoja tänav 4-6, **T** 644 8767. *Thu-Tue 1030-1800, closed Wed. 15 EEK. Free with Tallinn Card. Map 2, H5, p253*

Once the city prison, this intimate 14th-century building, with cool white walls and a grey stone floor, offers a compelling glimpse of what Tallinn and rural Estonia looked like in the early days of photography. The collection includes sepia photos of wheat, spinning wheels and round-faced country folk, stark Independence War images of corpses in the snow, pictures of Harju street and the fabled Golden Lion Hotel before the 1944 bombing and shots of a zeppelin gliding above the city. One of the most striking images is that of the French balloonist Charles Leroux, tangled in the strings of his hot-air balloon, moustache impeccable even in death, after his botched attempt to fly over the Bay of Tallinn in 1889. The patent for the Minox miniature spy camera, invented in Estonia by Walter Zapp and produced in Riga in 1938, is also on display.

Niguliste Muuseum-Kontserdisaal (Niguliste Museum and Concert Hall)

Niguliste 3, **T** 631 4330, www.ekm.ee. *Wed-Sun 1000-1700. 35 EEK. Free with Tallinn Card. Map 2, I4, p253*

Just southwest of Raekoja down Harju street, you will come to a solid-looking church set back from the main street, with modern stained glass lending an orange-pink glow to its light, white interior. It was built by seafaring merchants from Westphalia who settled in the area in 1230. Niguliste also has an impressive permanent collection of church art, the star attraction being the fragment of the Lübeck master Berndt Notke's *meisterwerk*, the *Danse Macabre*, which depicts Death as a leering skeleton, dancing in grotesque fashion with a pope, an emperor, an empress, a cardinal and a king. Among the other works, look out for the highly expressive sculpture of St George triumphantly stamping on the head of the dragon (you can't help feeling sorry for the beast, such is the killer's expression); the wooden sculpture of St Christopher, with luscious curly hair; and Lübeck artist Hermann Rode's late-15th-century altarpiece devoted to the life of St Nicholas, in which the lurching ship highlights the saint's role as patron of seamen and merchants. Niguliste is also one of the city's flagship concert venues, thanks in part to its superb organ. Outside, a stone monument to the Estonian writer **Eduard Vilde** (1865-1933) depicts scenes from his novels and plays.

Rüütli street

Map 2, J3, p253

This is one of the city's prettiest streets. A plaque at number 22 marks the birthplace of artist Michel Sittow in 1469. Sittow studied painting with Hans Memling in Flanders and was a sought- after portraitist in several European courts, including those in Denmark, France and Spain. Sadly, the building is in urgent need of repair.

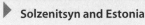

Solzenitsyn and Estonia

In *The Gulag Archipelago*, Solzenitsyn describes how fate brought him together with fellow prisoner Arnold Susi, a lawyer from Tallinn. "He [Susi] breathed a completely different sort of air, and he talked to me enthusiastically about his own world, and that world was Estonia and democracy. And although it had never occurred to me before to take an interest in Estonia – still less in bourgeois democracy – I listened and listened to his loving stories about the twenty free years of that reticent, hard-working, small nation of big men with their slow, solid ways. I listened to the principles of the Estonian constitution drawn from the best European experience and how it had been worked out by their single chamber parliament of a hundred deputies. And although I didn't know why, I began to be attracted by it all and to store it all away as part of my experience."

At the corner of Dunkri and Rataskaevu stands **Cat's Well**, once the main source of water for the city, a disturbing thought given that some locals believed the only way to prevent an evil spirit that lurked within from drying up all Tallinn's wells was to hurl stray cats into the water.

Rootsi-Mihkli Kirik (St Michael's Swedish Church)

Ruutli 7/9, **T** 644 1938, www.svenskakyrkanitallinn.com. *Daily 1000-1800, services in Swedish Sun 1200. Map 2, K4, p253*

This appropriately sparse Lutheran church was built as a hospital and almshouse in the 16th century. It served a Swedish congregation from 1733 until the Second World War, when most Swedes fled to their homeland. Used as a sports hall during the Soviet occupation, it was returned to the re-established Swedish congregation in 1992.

Harju street
Map 2, K4, J5, p253

A plaque marks the ruins and gaping bomb site created by a
Soviet air raid in March 1944. The raid, which for years the Russians
attributed to the Nazis, killed more than 600 people, gutted Niguliste
and destroyed 20,000 homes and numerous other buildings.
Although this is prime real estate, the consensus is that the ruins
should be preserved.

Sõprus Cinema
Vana-Posti 8, **T** 644 1919, www.kino.ee. *Map 2, J5, p253*

This wonderfully pompous Stalinist building, which now houses
the Hollywood nightclub, a fashionable lounge bar and an
arthouse cinema, was completed in 1955. For further details, see
Bars and clubs, p166 and p170, and Arts and entertainment, p175.

Teatri-ja Muusikamuuseum (Theatre and Music Museum)
Müürivahe 12, **T** 644 6407. *Wed-Sun 1000-1800. 20 EEK. Free with
Tallinn Card. Map 2, K5, p253*

Hardly anyone seems to come here but, frankly, they're missing
out. With an emphasis on music rather than theatre, the upstairs
display includes a superb collection of organs and automated
19th- and 20th-century music-making machines, one in the shape
of a boy with a piglet. If you're lucky, the pensioner on duty will
play them, filling the room with harmonies reminiscent of
fairgrounds. Pianists are invited to try the piano in the main hall, a
product of Tallinn's world-beating Estonia factory, which is used
for concerts. Ask for the English-language information sheet.

Carts and minds
Enterprising locals capitalize on the city's medieval heritage

Vanaturu kael (Old Market)
Map 2, I6, p253

This lively triangular crossroads, just off Raekoja plats, is the town's oldest market square. The warehouse where merchants once stashed their wares is now one of the city's flagship restaurants, *Olde Hansa*; stallholders in medieval dress, aided by Middle Ages music from the restaurant, do their best to re-create the heady atmosphere of the Hansa days.

★ Dominikaanlaste Klooster (Dominican Monastery)
Vene 16, **T** 644 4606. *May-Sep daily 0930-1800. 45 EEK. Free with Tallinn Card. Map 2, G7, p253*

Dating back to 1246, St Catherine's Monastery is the city's oldest intact building. On its completion in the 15th century, it was also the largest church in town. The gloomy but atmospheric monastery remains are well worth a visit, not least for the stone carvings displayed in the cloister.

Next to the monastery is the city's most intimate alley, the narrow **Katariina käik** (St Catherine's passageway), with overhead vaulting, wrought-iron lamps and workshops where you can watch artisans making jewellery, pottery and stained glass. Several gravestones from St Catherine's line its walls: the first, dated 1381, is the most unusual, as it commemorates a woman, Kuningunde Schottelmundt, and was carved at a time when women were not considered important enough to merit individual tombs. It is thought that she was the much-loved young wife of an important city figure; look carefully and you will see the fur trimming of her cape and pointy shoes.

Peeter-Pauli Kirik (St Peter and St Paul's Church)

Vene 18, **T** 644 6367 *Open with advance notification and during services. Map 2, G7, p253*

This pristine yellow-and-cream Catholic church was built on the site of St Catherine's refectory by the St Petersburg-based architect Carlo Rossi in 1845. Today it serves Estonia's minority Catholic population, as well as the Polish and Lithuanian communities.

Tallinna Linnamuuseum (Tallinn City Museum)

Vene 17, **T** 644 6553, www.linnamuuseum.ee *Mar-Oct Wed-Mon 1030-1800, Nov-Feb Wed-Mon 1100-1700. 35 EEK, concessions 10 EEK. Free with Tallinn Card. Map 2, F7, p252*

Housed in a handsome yellow merchant's house, the City Museum is an excellent introduction to the history of Tallinn, from the earliest settlements to the Singing Revolution. In the Hanseatic section, a soundtrack of trotting horses, tolling bells, lapping water and mooing cows takes you back to the days when furs, flax, wax, honey and hemp passed westwards through the port, while salt, cloth, herring, spices, wine and metals went east. Tallinn's main exports were limestone and grain. On the top floor, you can watch films of pre-war Tallinn and footage of the events that led up to the Singing Revolution, although the latter involves an eternity of speeches. Behind a panel of Soviet propaganda material, you'll find a second panel giving a more realistic depiction of what Soviet rule entailed, with pictures of the pre-war president and prime minister before and after their imprisonment. During the Second World War alone, Estonia lost more than 200,000 of its people through death, repression and flight to the west. One of the prize exhibits is an uplifting photograph of an elderly, bespectacled man sitting on the pedestal of Lenin's statue on present-day Rävala street. The date is 23 August 1991, and the statue has just been removed; arms outstretched and head thrown back, he's little short of ecstatic.

Nikolai Imetegija Kirik
(Church of St Nicholas the Miracle Worker)
Vene 24, **T** 644 1945. *Services in Russian Fri 1000, Sat 0930 and 1800, Sun 0930. Map 2, F7, p252*

Many Russian Orthodox believers will tell you that this beautifully proportioned, neatly domed neoclassical structure (built in the 1820s) has a much more spiritual feel than the portentous and overblown Nevsky Cathedral. Back in medieval times, a Russian church was built on nearby Sulevimägi for the Novgorod merchants who settled in this neighbourhood.

Viru
Map 2, E-F7, p252

From Vene, take Munga, then turn right onto Müürivahe, with its rough-hewn ramparts, past 'Knitting Wall', named for its stalls selling all manner of warm-looking woollies, to the twin towers of the

Rampart rambles

Given the number of sieges, attacks and aerial bombardments Tallinn has endured, it's little short of miraculous that 80% of the city fortifications, including 29 towers and the ruins of another three, have survived. The bumpy limestone walls, splashed with orange-topped turrets, are the city's most distinctive feature, a reminder that this was once one of the most impregnable strongholds in northern Europe. The first fortifications probably date back to the second half of the 13th century, but most of what you see today was built between 1300 and 1500. The stretch between the oldest towers, Nunne, Sauna and Kuldjala, is open to the public in summer (entrance on Vaike-Kloostri, under the tower, Map 2, E4, Mon-Fri 1200-1900, Sat and Sun 1100-1600). Less official, but more exciting, is a stroll from the Hellemann Tower, reached via the Kinomaja (Müürivahe 50, p64). From the sloping walkway, you can savour splendid views of Oleviste and Niguliste churches and the wonky angles of the rooftops below through the tiny defence windows. On Toompea, you can walk from the Megede (Maiden Tower, p45) to the Tallitorn (Stable Tower).

15th-century Viru Gate. After the construction of this section of the city wall, together with the gate, in the 16th century, merchants began moving to Viru street, which had previously been outside the city walls. This was the city's most fashionable, glamorous street in the 1920s and 1930s; today, it's Tallinn's answer to Oxford Street. Commercial, touristy and depressingly unmedieval, it's a favourite haunt of pickpockets. Its main architectural attraction is the steel, glass, wood and stone De La Gardie shopping centre.

Tallinn was further fortified in the 16th century with earthen embankments and ramparts. In the 17th century, the Swedes planned to surround the city with 12 bastions, but only a handful were built. For Peter the Great, Tallinn's strategic importance lay at sea and, following Russia's decision to strike Tallinn off the list of fortified towns in the mid-19th century, the bastions were handed over to the municipality, which had the good sense to turn them into parks and public gardens. The only surviving scraps of the Swedish bastions are Rannavärav, Harju and Linda hills. Rannavärav, a rather neglected patch of green just right of Paks Margareta, was once a rose garden, then an open-air theatre for Soviet troops. One of the best views of the city's towers is from Rannamäe, west of the city, while the loveliest stretch of reclaimed parkland runs from the manicured Tornide Väljak (Square of Towers), between Rannamäe tee and the Old Town (reach it via Suurtuki street), to the more romantic, rambling area around Šnelli Pond. Named after a local gardener, the pond is all that remains of the medieval moat. Bear in mind that pickpockets can be a problem here.

Pikk tänav
Map 2, F5-B7, p252

On the other side of Town Hall Square is Pikk tänav (Long street), known as the 'street of guilds'. In the Middle Ages, it was one of the city's most important thoroughfares, as it led from the trading centre all the way to the sea. It was natural that the guilds, precursors of today's trade unions, should settle here.

At Pikk 20, you'll find the neo-Gothic **St Canute's Guildhouse**, now used for contemporary dance. The building

Bachelor pad

Pikk street was once home to the Brotherhood of Blackheads, a guild composed of single men renowned for their parties.

dates back to the mid-19th century, but the guild was first mentioned in 1326 as an association for German goldsmiths, tailors, bakers and shoemakers. The Soviet takeover of Estonia in 1940 was plotted at the pink **Russian Embassy** building, across the way (Pikk 19). Pause to admire the Jugendstil façade with ornate Egyptian motifs at Pikk 18.

Further along, the brightly painted green, red and gold door belongs to the house of the **Brotherhood of the Blackheads** (Pikk 26). This is Tallinn's only Renaissance façade, carved by master mason Arendt Passer in 1587. The Blackheads, whose patron saint was the African St Mauritius (his profile is visible above the entrance) were an association of Baltic German bachelor merchants, goldsmiths and intellectuals, founded in 1399 and disbanded only after the Soviet takeover in 1940. Members were keen patrons of the arts and organized some of Tallinn's wildest parties. The neighbouring house (Pikk 24) belonged to the **Guild of Saint Olaf's**, founded in the 13th century for non-German craftsmen, including Estonians, who plied less prestigious trades: carpenters, boatmen, bell-ringers and gravediggers.

The **Interior Ministry building** (Pikk 59) was the headquarters of the NKVD (later the KGB) during the Soviet occupation. The basement rooms were used for torture and executions, hence the bricked-up windows. "Here," reads the simple plaque outside, "began the road to suffering for thousands of Estonians." The building is on the corner of Pagari (Bakers) street, home to bakeries in medieval times. The **Three Sisters**, an imposing 15th-century trio of lemon-and-cream merchants' houses towards the end of Pikk (beginning at number 71), is now a boutique hotel.

Eesti Ajaloomuuseum (Estonian History Museum)
Pikk 17, Great Guild Hall, **T** 641 1630. *Thu-Tue 1100-1800. 15 EEK. Free with Tallinn Card. Map 2, H2, p253*

Nobs and knockers
A detail from the façade of the Great Guild, home to the city's most influential group of merchants.

It's worth the price of admission just to see the high-vaulted interior of what was once the home of the city's wealthiest merchants. The museum houses eclectic temporary shows (such as weaponry) and a permanent display that spans early history and the 19th century. The coin room, meanwhile, has examples of hard currency from as far back as the Viking Age right through to those of the pre-war republic of Estonia.

Views

Best

- City wall towers from Rannamäe tee, p56.
- Oleviste spire, p61.
- Estonian Maritime Museum, p63.
- Television tower, p84.
- Paljassaare peninsula, p86.

★ Pühavaimu (Church of the Holy Ghost)

Pühavaimu 2, **T** 644 1487, www.eelk.ee. *Services on Sun in Estonian (1000) and English (1500).10 EEK entry outside these hours. Free with Tallinn Card. Map 2, G6, p253*

There's a refreshing lack of pomp about this prodigiously pretty whitewashed church, erected for a poor congregation and completed in 1360. It acquired an alluring copper spire following a fire in 2002. Formerly an almshouse church, it served the Estonian congregation and was the first church where sermons were given in Estonian; one of its preachers, Johan Koell, composed the first book in Estonian, a translation of the Lutheran catechism (1535). The only hint of flamboyance on Pühavaimu's façade is the city's oldest public clock, carved by Christian Ackermann in the 17th century. The interior has a hushed, intimate feel and one of the city's most prized medieval works of art, the 15th-century altar by Berndt Notke (1483). The Renaissance pulpit is Tallinn's most ancient.

★ Oleviste Kirik (Saint Olaf's church)

Pikk 48, **T** 641 2241. *Estonian-language services Sun 1000 and 1200; spire open Apr-Oct 100-1800, 25 EEK. Free with Tallinn Card. Map 2, C7, p252*

First cited in 1267, Oleviste was once renowned as the tallest building in the world. Its soaring spire was an important orientation point for seamen; more recently, the KGB used it to send radio transmissions. As a result of reconstruction in 1820, the original 159-m spire dwindled to 124 m, but it is still one of the most impressive sights on Tallinn's skyline, and the views of the Old Town, Toompea and the city wall from the viewing platform at its base are breathtaking. A recent repainting has left it dazzlingly white, a kind of architectural Gandalf. The church, which today belongs to a Baptist congregation, was built for Scandinavian merchants and named after the Norwegian king Olaf Haraldson. Its construction has spawned a host of unlikely tales: in the most popular, a mysterious mason offered to build the church for free if the city's authorities could discover his name. They couldn't, of course, until the 11th hour, when, in the face of financial ruin, a local worthy overheard the architect's wife comforting their young child with a song about how the father (Olev, naturally) would soon be home with wealth beyond their wildest dreams. When the worthy called up to Olev, the master builder was so shocked that he fell to his death; a serpent and a toad, sure signs of Satan's influence, crawled out of his mouth. A delicately carved cenotaph outside the church depicts a skeleton with a toad on its chest and a serpent around its skull.

Suur Rannavärav and Paks Margareeta (The Great Coast Gate and Fat Margaret's Tower)
End of Pikk. *Map 2, A8, p252*

In medieval times, the harbour lay just beyond the city wall. Since then, the land has risen by about 2 mm a year, hence the new shoreline. Built in the 14th century, the sea gate was restructured and refortified in the early 16th century, its most impressive addition being a stocky cannon tower with walls so stout that it later acquired the nickname of Paks Margareeta (Fat Margaret). In Tsarist times, it was a jail for political prisoners, which is why a mob set it alight during the Russian Revolution.

Estonian Maritime Museum

Paks Margareeta, Pikk 70, **T** 641 1408. *Wed-Sun, 1000-1800, closed Mon-Tue. 25 EEK, free with Tallinn Card. Map 2, A8, p252*

Fat Margaret is now a museum devoted to Estonia's long and deep association with the sea. On display are models of ships, ancient fishing equipment and artefacts salvaged from wrecks; none of them, however, can hold a candle to the building itself, a vast conical structure that must have inspired unshakeable confidence in those assigned to defend it. As you climb from floor to floor, look through the arrow slits and windows – or try to, as the walls are 6 m thick. Climb the external stairs for an unusual view of the Old Town and the sea from the wind-lashed rooftop terrace.

Outside, a plaque unveiled by Prince Andrew in 1998 commemorates British naval support for Estonian forces in the Independence War. Beyond the sea gate, on the right, is another memorial, this time to the 850 people who died when the Estonia ferry went down on its way to Stockholm on 28 September 1994. The two arcs can be taken to represent the broken line between Tallinn and Stockholm, or life cut short.

★ Tarbekunstimuuseum (Applied Arts Museum)

Lai 17, **T** 641 4600. *Wed-Sun 1100-1800. 20 EEK. Free with Tallinn Card. Map 2, E5, p252*

Housed in a former granary, storehouse and powder magazine, this intelligently designed museum is one of the city's best. Three floors are devoted to ceramics, glassware, leather, metalwork, textiles and jewellery, all of which are strong traditions in Estonia. You may be tempted to walk away with half the stuff on show; instead, study the displays and note the names to look out for in the city's more upmarket shops.

Tervishoiumuuseum (Health Museum)

Lai 30, **T** 641 1730/641 1732, www.tervishoiumuuseum.ee. *Tue-Sat 1100-1800. 20 EEK, free with Tallinn Card. Map 2, E5, p252*

Tallinn is not short of didactic museums, and this is no exception. There's a disturbingly large model of a tongue, while the interactive displays might keep children entertained. If you've come here for a weekend of hedonism, however, images of cirrhosis-ravaged livers and graphic pictures of the effects of sexual diseases are probably the last thing you want to see.

Issanda Muutmise Peakirik (Church of the Transfiguration of our Lord)

Suur-Kloostri 14, **T** 646 4003. *Sun and on request. Map 2, E4, p252*

Originally the church of the Cistercian nunnery, then the Swedish army, this became the Russian garrison church in the 1720s. Inside, you can see an iconostasis donated by Peter the Great.

Uus (New street)
Map 2, D-H8, p252-3

If Lai is the 'street of theatres', Uus is the street of the unexpected. New street (the name comes from its location just outside the city wall) is beautiful and bizarre in equal measure. The arrestingly pretty **Lithuanian Embassy** (Uus 15) is a uniquely flamboyant example of Tallinn baroque. Across the way, a plaque at Uus 10 tells you that Dostoevsky stayed here in 1840. Further down, past antiquarian bookshops and antiques stores, you will come to the slightly dilapidated **Kinomaja** (Cinema House, Uus 3), with its curious turquoise, pink and orange trimmings and equally curious floral weathervane. Step inside to climb Hellemann Tower (p56).

Mine Museum

Uus 37, **T** 641 1004. *Apr-Sep Wed-Sun 1000-1800, Oct-Mar Wed-Sun 0900-1700. 15 EEK. Free with Tallinn Card. Map 2, B8, p252*

At the north end of Uus, the air begins to bristle with the sound of marching music. Its source is the Mine Museum, a chilling reminder of what lies beneath the Baltic Sea. The deactivated mines on display here have been fished out of the Bay of Tallinn or brought in from the Estonian islands. One German device was neutralized by farmers on the island of Muhu, then used as a bowl. Ask the unnervingly enthusiastic staff whether there are any more mines in the bay and you will be gleefully told that a good 20 or so arrive here every year.

Kesklinn

After the charms of the Old Town, sprawling Vabaduse väljak, with an ugly car park at its heart, is almost shocking. On closer inspection, however, its eclectic muddle of pre- and post-war buildings includes some of the city's finest 20th-century architecture. East of Vabaduse are bustling arteries Pärnu maantee and Estonia puiestee, home of the city's beloved opera house. To the west stands stolid Kaarli Kirik (Charles Church), built during the Tsarist period as a strong Estonian riposte to the Russian dominance of Nevsky Cathedral. Many of the more business-oriented hotels and banks can be found between Vabaduse and Liivalaia (Dune street), to the south. The first upmarket department store to arrive in the 1990s, the Finnish-run Stockmann, sprung up here, giving its name to the eastern end of the street. Although the whole area is prosaically labelled Kesklinn (town centre), the individual neighbourhoods have more poetic names, such as Onion Village.

▶▶ *See Sleeping p131, Eating and drinking p154, Bars and clubs p170*

◉ Sights

Vabaduse väljak (Freedom Square)
Map 3, G2, p255

In medieval days, this square was a hay and wood market, from which cattle were led through Karja ('herd') Gate into the Old Town. To celebrate the 200th anniversary of Russian rule in 1910, the square was named Peetri plats (Peter Square) and a bronze statue of Peter the Great was erected. Peter was pulled down during the early years of Estonian independence, when the square was renamed Freedom Square, and the base of the statue was used to mint the new republic's five-cent coins. Most of the buildings on the square were erected in the 1920s and 1930s. On the south side, the **Gloria Palace Cinema** (1926), with its sculpted wreaths, grapes and lions, is now the **Russian Drama Theatre**. The grimy **Palace Hotel**, unofficial headquarters for foreign diplomats during the heady days of the early 1990s, was built in the mid-1930s. The clinker-clad, expressionist-style **City Government Building** (number 7), with lantern carriers on the façade, raised brick patterns and sculpted foliage, is stunning at night, when the central stairwell is illuminated. On the north side are the pink functionalist **Art Building**, its simplicity tempered by the protruding square of glass at the centre of its façade, and the neighbouring Stalinist structure, decorated with sculpted flames and now home to the the Association of Artists. The lonesome-looking, apricot-coloured **Jaani Kirik** (St John's Church) was built in the 1860s for the Lutheran congregation. The newest building here is the slim, wavy, glass-panelled **Kawe Plaza**. The Freedom Clock, with its blue and white columns, shows the passing of time since Independence in 1918.

Leading south from Vabaduse is **Roosikrantsi** (Rosary street), so named because this was where prisoners were led out of town to the gallows. One of the loveliest buildings, halfway down at number 15, is a Jugendstil white-and-orange apartment house with curved balconies. Join traffic-heavy Pärnu maantee and it's a five-minute walk to Christian Luther's Villa (number 67), one of the finest examples of Jugendstil in Estonia. Formerly the home of a plywood magnate, it is now the registry office.

National Library

Tõnismägi 2, **T** 630 7150. *Sep-Jun Mon-Fri 1000-2000, Sat 1100-1800, Jul-Aug Mon-Fri 1200-1900. Day pass 5 EEK. Free with Tallinn Card. Map 3, J-I1, p255*

This imposing limestone structure, with tinted windows, is a masterpiece of Soviet-Estonian architecture. Although some locals say it's oppressive and smacks of the Soviet era, it is impressive and uplifting inside, with vaulting giving an intimate feel to its hugeness, and the stained-glass window is arresting. Climbing the smooth, broad steps, you'd swear they were marble; they are in fact a polished version of its poor cousin, the local limestone.

Kaarli Kirik

Toompuiestee 4, **T** 611 9011. *Services in Estonian Sun 1000. Map 3, H1, p255*

The yellowy limestone neo-Romanesque church was completed in 1882 on the site of a former wooden church of the same name. It's home to the first fresco in Estonian art history, Johann Köler's *Come to Me*, and to one of the country's most powerful organs.

! Artists interested in residencies in Tallinn should check out the newly renovated studio of the Estonian Artists' Association, Vabaduse 6, 627 3630, www.eaa.ee.

Museum of Occupations

Toompea 8, **T** 668 0250, www.okupatsioon.ee. *Tue-Sun 1100-1800. 10 EEK. Free with Tallinn Card. Map 3, H1, p255*

This large, modern display traces the country's history from the Second World War to the end of the Soviet occupation in 1991. Boats and piles of suitcases in the hall evoke the flight and deportation of Estonians during the war, but the display cases containing boots, shoes and army uniform paraphernalia are a little old-fashioned. The chief draw is the black and white Second World War film footage; English commentary is available (and wryly entertaining).

Sakala
Map 3, H5, p255

Head back east to Pärnu maantee (a good five minutes' walk) and south onto Rävala puiestee, where you will be struck by the self-important limestone **Sakala Conference Centre** (number 12), once the Political Education Centre for the Estonian Communist Party. Incongruously church-like in design, with buttresses and a chunky tower, it was dubbed 'Karl's Cathedral' in Soviet times, after Karl Vaino, the party chief. The future of the building remains uncertain

Sakala leads northeast into **Sibulaküla** (Onion Village), named after the Russian civil servants who received plots of land here in the 18th century and grew these all-important vegetables. **Islandi Square** is named in honour of Iceland, the first country to recognize Estonia's renewed independence in 1991.

Eesti Panga Muuseum (Estonian Bank Museum)

Estonia puiestee 11, **T** 668 0760. *Wed-Fri 1200-1700. Free. Map 3, H4, p255*

Housed in the neo-Gothic Bank Building (1902-1904), topped with a lion-shaped weather vane and mosaics of Tallinn's spires on its red-brick façade, this museum is devoted to the various currencies that have been in use in Estonia, from Tsarist days to the euro age. The wax figures of those who have appeared on Estonian banknotes are eerily lifelike, enough to deceive you into thinking that you are not, as in so many museums in Tallinn, the only visitor.

Estonia Theatre and Estonia Concert Hall

Estonia puiestee 4, **T** 626 0260. *Box office 1200-1900. Map 2, K9, p253*

These twin cream-and-yellow neoclassical buildings, with pagoda-style green-tiled roofs and decorative urns, were erected – despite protests from the Tsarist authorities – with money donated by Estonians, for whom the creation of a national theatre was of enormous significance. An impoverished poet, Juhan Liiv, famously donated his sole possession, the coat from his back, which he reverently laid on the ground outside. The theatre was built on a marketplace where, in 1905, scores of Estonian demonstrators were massacred by Tsarist troops.

On nearby **Georg Otsa street**, there is a monument to the Tallinn teachers and students who lost their lives during the Independence War. Destroyed by the Soviets in 1940 (students and teachers who protested were arrested, and some were never seen again), it was replaced in 1993.

Estonian Drama Theatre

Pärnu maantee 5, **T** 644 3976, www.dramateater.ee. *Closed in August. Map 3, G4, p255*

Originally the German Theatre (1910), this lovely venue with green trimmings and stretched oval windows was built in romantic

Jugendstil style. Across the way, at Pärnu maantee 10, stands a vast bank and apartment building with staggeringly steep entrance steps designed by the Finnish architect Eliel Saarinen.

Tatari
Map 3, H-I8-9, p255

Just south of All-Linn is the neighbourhood of **Tatari**, named after the Russian troops who were based here during the Livonian War. Amid the steel and glass that characterizes much of the Kesklinn, the somewhat dilapidated 19th-century wooden houses between Tatari and Süda streets, with their peaceful courtyards and gardens, come as something of a relief.

It's a good 10-minute walk down to **Liivalaia**, where the most interesting sights are at the eastern end, near Tartu maantee. The Stockmann department store has a lumpen exterior, but its bright interior is an eloquent symbol of Estonia's Scandinavian orientation. Although the street was bombed beyond recognition in the Second World War, a handful of wooden buildings give a sense of how beautiful it once was: the house with a blue turret on the corner of Liivalaia and Lennuki, and, across the street, the small, green onion-domed **Church of Our Lady of Kazan** (Liivalaia 38, **T** 660 7990; *0900-1400*), the oldest preserved wooden church in Tallinn, built in 1721.

At the corner of Liivalaia and Tartu maantee stands **Stalin's Palace** (Tartu maantee 24, built 1954), a pompous and unmistakably Stalinist 'wedding cake', its church-like spire topped with laurel wreath and pointed star. It now houses luxury apartments.

Harbour and around

The bustling harbour has a buzzing border feel. Like a Calais of the north, it is awash with supermarkets and tacky shops selling everything from fake-looking Soviet memorabilia to off-the-peg wedding dresses. The reason Finns flock here, other than to stock up on cheap alcohol, is to attend spas and high-tech, relatively inexpensive dental surgeries. The Rotermann Quarter, located between the Old Town and the harbour, is an old industrial area of limestone and brick buildings. In the 1980s, it was frequented by Finnish architecture students, having acquired cult status as the setting of Tarkovsky's film Stalker. *In the 1990s, there was much debate about how to develop this area: in the absence of a clear plan, money talked, leading to the rapid erection of architectural eyesores. The demolition of the industrial ruins where* Stalker *was filmed made way for the Metropole Hotel. Luckily, this trend was nipped in the bud, and today the area is prime real estate, with fashionable restaurants, clubs and stylish modern buildings appearing alongside the booze shops and casinos on Mere puiestee.*
▸▸ *See Sleeping p132, Eating and drinking p156, Bars and clubs p172*

◉ Sights

**Eesti Arhitektuurimuuseum
(Museum of Estonian Architecture)**
Rotermann Salt Storage, Ahtri 2, **T** 625 7006/7000, www.arhitek
tuurimuuseum.ee. *Wed-Fri 1200-2000, Sat and Sun 1100-1800.
Closed Mon-Tue. 30 EEK. Free with Tallinn Card. Map 3, C6, p254*

Appropriately enough, the city's most hotly contested architectural battleground is now home to the city's Museum of Architecture. This handsome, triangular-roofed limestone storage depot was built in 1908 for Christian Barthold Rotermann, an Estonian industrialist, who made a fortune out of a distillery, sugar mill and food production. Today, the building hosts intelligently presented, high-quality art and architecture exhibitions, and is used for happening house parties and ambassadorial farewells.

Church of St Simeon and the Prophetess Hanna

Ahtri 5, **T** 644 5744/509 3607, www.eoc.ee. *Services Sat 1700 and Sun 1000. Map 3, C8, p254*

With a glistening copper onion dome and lace wood trimming, this beautiful little church seems entirely out of place in the blighted industrial wasteland that surrounds it. Built in the 18th century to serve Russian seamen, it was then so close to the sea that flotsam and jetsam from shipwrecks was reputedly used to reinforce the foundations. A new synagogue is opens on Karu street in 2006; the old one was bombed by the Russians during the Second World War.

Russian Cultural Centre

Mere puiestee 5. *Map 3, D5, p254*

Formerly the Grand Marina Cinema, built in 1912 to entertain the large community of Tsarist troops in Tallinn, this was the largest cinema in the Tsarist empire. Destroyed during the Second World War, it was rebuilt in self-important Stalinist style in the 1950s, when it acquired its cream-and-orange neoclassical façade, complete with hammer and sickle. A recreational club for Soviet naval officers, it was given to the Russian-speaking community after the restoration of independence. After a dodgy start – the administration had Russian mafia links and was the subject of scandal and disappearing funds (one of its directors resigned and was then shot, along with his son) – things have calmed down. In **St Canute's Garden**, next to the northern wing of the centre, there is a bust of Dostoevsky, who visited Tallinn when his brother was serving in the Tsarist army here.

Across the street stands **Rotermann's distillery**, now home to the Scotland Yard bar. At the end of the 19th century, this was the first factory building in Estonia to install electricity. **Rotermann's Market Centre**, established by the tycoon's father, now houses food and clothes shops, as well as 24-hour off-licences.

Viru väljak
Map 3, E5, p254

Once the tallest building in the land, the **Viru Hotel** (1972) was built by Finns, with Finnish materials, as an Intourist hotel. It is hard to imagine that this lumpy brown-and-white high-rise was once a symbol of luxury, that microphones were hidden in the rooms and that Tallinners were not allowed inside in case they mixed with the supposedly dangerous westerners. Now owned by a Finnish group, it's a favourite stopover for the cousins from across the water. A recent renovation has made it less Soviet and more mundane.

Tammsaare Park
Between Pärnu maantee and Estonia puiestee. *Map 3, F5, p254*

West of Viru lies a park established in 1948 on a former bombsite, and used by many Tallinners to go in and out of the Old Town. It was originally called Stalin Square, then, after his death, 16th October Park but, after the monument to the novelist Anton Tammsaare was erected in 1978 (see Kadriorg, below), it unofficially acquired his name. Locals say that Tammsaare's expression, a combination of reflectiveness, scepticism and resignation, is deeply Estonian.

Kadriorg

An aristocratic seaside resort in Tsarist times, this leafy district has a dignified, even haughty, air, as befits the site of Peter the Great's summer palace and the Estonian president's official residence. It is home to several foreign embassies and some of Tallinn's wealthiest businessmen. Come the weekend, Tallinners flock to 'Catherine's Vale' (named after Peter's wife, Catherine I) to amble through romantic parkland and groves of lindens and limes, or admire the painted wooden houses and streamlined Functionalist apartment blocks. Adding to the refined feel, several streets are named after leading cultural figures, some of whom lived here and are honoured in local museums. Kadriorg is now one of the city's cultural hubs, with a vast new art museum. It's also the site of the huge Song Festival Grounds, one of the cradles of the Singing Revolution.
▸▸ *See Sleeping p134, Eating and drinking p157*

Getting there: take tram 1 or 3 to Kadriorg Park or bus 35 and 34 from Viru väljak to J Poska.

Song Festival Grounds

Narva maantee 95, **T** 611 2102, www.lauluvaljak.ee. *Free. Buses 1, 1A, 5, 8, 34, 38 to Lauluväljak; buses 1,19, 29, 35, 44, 60, 63 to Lasnamägi. Map 1, D9, p251*

Every Estonian town has its song bowl, but none has anything to compare with this vast venue, where 300,000 people gave voice to their discontent at Soviet occupation in 1988, sparking the Singing Revolution. The stage, with its imposing shell of pinewood and steel, can hold up to 30,000 singers and faces a steepish slope from where there are fine sea views. The National Song and Dance Festival takes place only once every five years, so the venue is also used for rock and classical concerts, the popular summer beer festival and several fairs (see Festivals and events, p185).

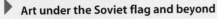

▶ Art under the Soviet flag and beyond

Estonian artists did not make their mark until the late 19th century, with painter Johann Köler and sculptor August Weizenberg. In the 20th century, many Estonian painters moved to western Europe and brought the dynamism of its art back home. Social realism officially dominated the Soviet era, when sculpture was often more interesting than painting. Abstractionism, exemplified by Ado Lill and Raul Meel, was rediscovered in the 1960s as a reaction against figurative art. Happenings, Surrealism, Land Art and Pop Art also found followers.

Post-1991, Estonia has been officially represented at the Venice Biennale. The best known video artists are Jaan Toomik and Ene-Liis Semper, Raoul Kurvitz, Marco Laimre and Kai Kaljo. Photographers include Peeter Laurits, Herkki-Erich Merila, Mark Raidpere and Liina Siib.

The **Centre of Contemporary Arts**, Vabaduse väljak 6, **T** 631 4050, www.cca.ee, has an information centre and library. You could also visit **Galerii-G**, Vasadvse Valjak 6, **T** 644 9620; and **Linnagalerii**, Harju 13, **T** 644 1388.

★ Kadriorg Palace

Weizenbergi 37, **T** 606 6400, www.ekm.ee/kadriorg. *Tue-Sun 1000-1700, closed Mon; Oct-Apr also closed Tue. 45 EEK. Free with Tallinn Card. Tram 1 and 3.* *Kadriorg detail map 1, G11, p251*

Designed in 1718 for Peter the Great by Italian architect Nicolo Michetti (who built St Petersburg's Versailles-esque Peterhof Palace), this mulberry-coloured building with cream pillars and graceful oval windows is modest, sober baroque at its best. It is thought that Peter laid the first stone.

Today, it houses the Estonian Art Museum's foreign section. The collection includes works by Breughel the Younger, Cranach and Cuyp, as well as Russian portraiture and academic realist paintings. The setting is as fine as the collection, in particular the festive hall, with its sculpted seashells, fruits and garlands of oak leaves, as well as a relief depicting Poseidon (believed to be a representation of the Tsar, who won access to the Baltic Sea), and the glazed black- and white-tiled baroque heating stoves in the rooms.

Eesti Kunstimuuseumi (KUMU)

Weizenbergi 34/Valge1, **T** 644 9139, www.ekm.ee. *May-Sep Tue-Sun 1100-1800; Oct-Apr Wed-Sun 1100-1800. 75 EEK for all exhibits, 50 EEK for the permanent exhibition, 40 EEK for temporary shows. Free for children under 7. Kadriorg detail map, H12, p251*

This stunning new glass and concrete structure, amid revamped parkland, houses the new Estonian Art Museum. The permanent collection is a comprehensive survey of the nation's art, from the 18th century through Impressionism and post-war social realism to hyperrealism and contemporary work. It also hosts temporary shows devoted to international artists.

Mikkel Museum

Weizenbergi 28, **T** 606 6400, www.ekm.ee. *Wed-Sun 1100-1800. Closed Mon-Tue. 15 EEK. Free with Tallinn Card. Kadriorg detail map, G11, p251*

Born in 1907, Johannes Mikkel began amassing art treasures in pre-war Estonia, many left in the country when the Baltic Germans and Russian nobles fled the country in 1917-18; in the post-war era, he continued to collect, despite the obvious hurdles posed by the oppressive communist regime, by cultivating contacts all over the Soviet Union, notably in Georgia. "Art," he rather innocently put it, "has the magical ability of wandering to where it is loved."

In 1995, Mikkel donated his collection to the Estonian Art Museum and it is now displayed in the palace's former kitchen. Highlights include etchings by Rembrandt and Piranesi, a woodcut by Dürer and a fine collection of porcelain, including 18th-century decorative Chinese plates.

Peter the Great House Museum

Mäekalda 2, **T** 601 3136, www.linnamuuseum.ee. *May-Aug Wed-Sun 1100-1900; Sep-Apr Wed-Sun 1030-1700. 15 EEK, children 7 EEK. Free with Tallinn Card. Kadriorg detail map, G12, p251*

The great Tsar stayed in what he called his "cottage in the woods" before work on the much grander palace began. Inside, the modest living room, bedroom, dining room and kitchen are furnished with period items and a few of Peter's possessions.

The pink-and-white neoclassical **Residence of the President** (30a Weizenbergi) lies behind the palace. Further up and to the right stands the peeling orange former school building that is to house the new **Russian Museum**.

Eduard Vilde Memorial Museum

Roheline aas 3, **T** 601 3181. *Wed-Mon 1100-1700. 10 EEK. Free with Tallinn Card. Kadriorg detail map, H10, p251*

Housed in the pink palace governor's home, a kind of bonsai version of Kadriorg Palace, this museum celebrates the life and work of one of the nation's greatest writers. Post-independence, the Estonian government gave him the house where he spent the last years of his life, in recognition of his work.

Anton Hansen Tammsaare Museum

Koidula 12a, **T** 601 3232. *Wed-Mon 1000-1700. 10 EEK. Free with Tallinn Card. Kadriorg detail map, G9, p251*

This romantic, slightly tumbledown green wooden villa was the last residence of Tammsaare, best known for the five-part epic *Truth and Justice*. A bust in the garden shows the retiring writer looking characteristically reflective. Inside, you can visit his modest family flat, one of four in the building. You can see the maid's room, the 1930s-style dining room, the author's study and the lovely verandah, where, owing to stomach complications, Tammsaare would write standing up. Some of the exhibits are wonderfully evocative of pre-war Estonia, including the menu and orchestra programme for an evening at the celebrated *Kuldlovi* (Golden Lion) hotel, destroyed in the Soviet bombing raid of March 1944.

Russalka monument

Map 1, D8, p251

This moving sculpture of an angel looking out to sea commemorates the loss of 177 soldiers who drowned when the Russalka ('Mermaid') sank on its way to Finland in 1893. The rough rocks around the pedestal evoke waves on a stormy sea. In July 2003, the wreck of the vessel was found in the Finnish Gulf.

Pirita

The 20-minute coastal ride to Pirita, beside windswept pines and the silvery Bay of Tallinn, is one of northern Europe's most uplifting, with bracing sea air and unforgettable views of the compact city skyline. Pirita took shape as a resort in the early 20th century. The atmosphere of leisure and innocence, soon to be destroyed by the Second World War, is beautifully captured in Jaan Kross's short story

> ## Who's who in Kadriorg

Several leading figures have given their names to streets in Kadriorg in recognition of their contribution to Estonian cultural and public life:

F R Fahelmann (1798-1859) Scholar and collector of Estonian folk poetry.

Jaan Poska (1866-1920) The first Estonian mayor of Tallinn (1913-1917).

August Weizenberg (1873-1921) The first professional Estonian sculptor.

Johann Köler (1826-99) The first professional Estonian painter.

Lydia Koidula (1843-86) Beloved National Awakening poet, whose poem *Mu isamaa on minu arm* ("My Fatherland is my Love") was the unofficial anthem during the Soviet era.

The Wound, *in which a farewell dinner takes place in a Pirita restaurant against a backdrop of "the bay and the city lights beyond in the misty darkness". Today, the rich and famous, including supermodel Carmen Kass, buy, build or renovate villas here. One of the loveliest sights is the soaring gable of the 15th-century St Birgitta Convent, a ruin now, but far more aesthetically pleasing than the showcase marina complex built for the 1980 Olympics. Under Soviet occupation, the beach was a forbidden zone at night, carefully surveyed to ensure that nobody tried to escape to the West. Today, Pirita is a popular place for cycling, roller-blading and even surfing, while the Pirita valley offers delightful forest walks and rides.*

▸▸ *See Sleeping p134, Eating and drinking p158*

Getting there: Bus numbers 1, 1a, 8, 34, 34a, 38 and 99.

Maarjamäe Loss (Maarjamäe Castle)
Pirita tee 56, **T** 601 4535. *Wed-Sun 1100-1800. Closed Mon-Tue. 15 EEK. Free with Tallinn Card. Map 1, C9, p251*

Built on 'Mary's Hill' in 1874, the eccentric-looking summerhouse of a Russian count, Anatoli Orlov-Davydov, houses the 20th-century section of the Estonian History Museum. The main focus of the exhibition is the Estonian resistance movement and the Independence War, with plenty of photographs and newspaper clippings on show, though few captions in English.

Soviet War Memorial
Maarjamägi (next to Maarjamäe Loss). *Map 1, C9, p251*

This extraordinarily pompous concrete memorial (1975), with its soaring obelisk, is a mighty symbol of Soviet power and, as such, is hated by many Estonians. It commemorates the Soviet soldiers of the First and Second World Wars, but is also the site of a Nazi cemetery, which has been restored with funds from Germany. Climb to the top to appreciate the sheer scale of the place, as well as the superb vistas out to sea. Now sinking into a state of neglect, it has a certain romantic attraction for young couples and has even hosted very un-Soviet punk gigs.

Olympic Center
Regati puiestee 1. *Map 1, B9-10, p251*

Built to host the yachting regatta of the 1980 Olympics, this hulking complex includes a monumental and rather ugly spa hotel and a yacht harbour from where you can take a boat to the islands.

Russian Tallinn

Russian cultural history in Estonia stretches back almost 1000 years. Finno-Ugric people and Russians lived together for centuries, and social crossover and intermarriage would have been common. In the 16th century, political refugees found shelter in Estonia, as did the persecuted Orthodox Old Believers, who settled in northern and eastern Estonia and around Lake Peipsi. After the Livonian and Swedish-Polish wars, which left a depleted population, many Russian peasants moved to Estonia, as did people from Hungary and even some 100 families from Scotland. In the early 19th century, many Russians holidayed in Estonia. Pushkin's Cameroon-born great-grandfather, Hannibal, was favoured by Peter the Great, who made him military governor of Tallinn. Pushkin's wife had relatives near Tartu. Dostoevsky spent time in Tallinn, mostly gambling, and Estonian characters sometimes appear in his novels. Oleviste church pastor von Hun was the model for the great inquisitor in *The Brothers Karamazov*. Following the Russian Revolution of 1917, Estonia became one of the most important centres for icon painting and scholarship in the world.

Today, one of the city's coolest clubs, *Bon Bon*, has monthly Russian evenings, and one of Estonia's most famous bands, outside its own borders, are the Russian-speaking Ne Zhdali, who play at jazz festivals around the world. A museum devoted to Russian culture in Estonia, a project first mooted in 1931, is supposed to open before the end of the decade.

Pirita beach
Map 1, A10, p251

The official beach, 6 km east of Tallinn, lies just north of the mouth of the Pirita River and is backed by a shady forest of lofty, slender-stalked pines. Forever in search of silence, many Estonians shun Pirita, as it is the city's most popular beach, but don't let that put you off. There is plenty of space, and shallow water up to 500 m out makes it ideal for children and first-time surfers. (For details of surfing, bicycle and skate rental, and Pirita Marina, see Sports, p199.) From the beach, you could spend hours gazing at Tallinn's spiky skyline or watching the cruise ships come and go from Stockholm and Helsinki. On the beach, there are volleyball nets and swings but, bizarrely, few other facilities. Alcohol is prohibited on the beach, so nobody is prepared to open a kiosk.

Pirita River Valley
Map 1, B10-12, p251

Drift upstream alongside willows, rustling reeds, ducks and pines, and enjoy views of Saint Birgitta's noble gable and the brilliant white cross atop the modern convent next door. Rowboat and pedalo hire is available from Barrel BG Boats, Kloostri 6a, opposite the Olympic complex (see Sports, p201), and boat trips are free for holders of a Tallinn Card.

★ St Birgitta (Convent of St Bridget)
Kloostri 9, **T** 605 5044/5568. *Daily summer 1000-1800; Jan-Apr and Nov-Dec 1200-1600. 20 EEK. Free with Tallinn Card. Map 1, B10, p251*

The distinctive skeletal silhouette of this ruined convent is a spectacular sight. Founded in 1407 by a trio of widowed merchants and completed in 1436, its gable was a useful orientation point for seamen. Badly damaged by Ivan the Terrible's troops during the Livonian War, it was reduced to ruins by the end of the Northern War, when its stones were easy plunder for locals in search of building material. The remains have at last been carefully restored and the Brigittine nuns now live in an award-winning, modern building that also houses a guesthouse.

Metsakalmistu (Forest Cemetery)
On Kloostrimetsa tee, where the road forks. *Bus 34a, or 38 from Viru keskus. Map1, B12, p251*

Estonians bury their loved ones under trees, and this peaceful, sprawling cemetery – filled with the fragrant scent of pines, its paths strewn with needles and cones – is a quintessential resting place. Here you will find the graves of poetess Lydia Koidula (her remains were brought over from Kronstadt in 1946), chess champion Paul Keres, writer AH Tammsaare and the deported pre-war president, Konstantin Päts, reburied here in 1990.

Botanical Gardens
52 Kloostrimetsa tee, **T** 606 2666, www.tba.ee. *Daily 1100-1600; gardens until 1900 May-Sep. 40 EEK, pensioners 20 EEK, children under 7 and disabled free, family 60 EEK. No charge for the gardens. Bus 34 or 38 from Viru Keskus. Map 1, B12, p251*

Opened in 1961 on what was formerly President Päts' family farm in the Pirita valley, this is worth visiting for the romantic gardens alone. The woodlands, meadows and flower gardens have been

! During the Olympic Regatta in 1980, a gold medal went to a Finn. As the Finnish national anthem played, Estonians sang their own prohibited, pre-war national anthem (the words are different, but the melody is the same), much to the horror of the KGB, who could do nothing with so many Westerners present.

beautifully maintained, and wandering around here is a great way to recharge if you are tired of town. The only discordant note is struck by the inescapable Television Tower.

Teletörn (Television Tower)

Kloostrimetsa 58a, **T** 623 8250, www.teletorn.ee. *Daily 1000-0100, Galaxy restaurant 1200-2200. 50 EEK. Free with Tallinn Card. Buses 34 and 38. Map 1, B12, p251*

Somewhat dilapidated at its base, this soaring space-age tower opened on Revolution Day (7 November) in 1980 and is unmistakably Soviet. In August 1991, it was the scene of a tense stand-off between Soviet troops, who wanted to seize the tower, and Estonians. The Russians eventually withdrew. Take the wobbly-feeling lift up to the Galaxy restaurant, on the 170-m-high viewing platform, so dingy it almost hurts your eyes. Turn your attention instead to the panoramic view: telescopes zoom in on the Old Town, St Birgitta, the villas of Pirita and the vast spread of Lasnamäe. In fine weather, you should be able to see all the way to Helsinki.

Kalamaja and Kopli Bay

Kalamaja ('Fish House') has what can only be described as soul. Inhabited in prehistoric times by fishermen, it was home in the Middle Ages to a community of Estonians and Swedes, among them boatmen, fishermen and innkeepers. Balthasar Russow, the Baltic Dick Whittington, was born here, as was, centuries on, the author, Jaan Kross. Following the creation of the St Petersburg-Tallinn railway, several engineering works and factories were established in the neighbourhood, which also had the highest concentration of tinned spiced sprat production. Many of the street names are factory-related or whimsically inspired by Estonian folklore. Old

Kalamaja is fast shedding its reputation as a sad slum of dilapidated wooden tenements. First-time buyers and arty types, attracted by the charms of the houses and the area's proximity to the Old Town and sea, are moving in and restoring the tumbledown dwellings. To the northwest is the relatively poor neighbourhood of Kopli, which is emerging from a rough patch: its beach has been spruced up as part of the city's plans to make the area more desirable. At the furthest end of Kopli Bay, the open-air Rocca al Mare Museum, with its sea views, windmills and traditional peasant buildings, is ideal for picnics in fine weather or romantic trudges through winter snow.

▸▸ *See Sleeping p135, Eating and drinking p159, Bars and clubs, p172*

Sights

Tallinn Science and Technology Centre
Põhja puiestee 29, **T** 715 2650. *Jun-Sep Mon-Fri 1000-1700; Oct-May Mon-Fri 1000-1700, Sat 1200-1700. 35 EEK. Free with Tallinn Card. Map 3, A4, p254*

Housed in an old power station, this museum purports to examine the history of energy production from the Middle Ages to the new millennium. It's low-tech, and there are few English explanations, but children will relish the array of hands-on exhibits, and the lightning-conductor demonstrations are spectacular.

Jaama Turg (Railway Station Market)
Kopli 1. *Map 1, E5, p250*

Most Estonians say that this Russian-style market is a dump, but junk-lovers may stumble across unusual finds and clothes, not to mention dirt-cheap fruit and veg.

Suur Patarei
Suur Patarei street. *Map 1, D6, p250*

The former seafront prison crops up in the short stories of Jaan Kross, who, like so many Estonians, found himself here during the Second World War under the Nazi and/or Soviet occupations. In his short story *The Conspiracy*, he talks of the taunting "rushing of the sea in the background". To reach the prison, cross the old railway line and head seaward until you come to a long, white building with barbed wire and barred windows trimmed with red brick.

Paljassaare Peninsula
Bus 59 from Balti jaam. Map 1, A-B3-4, p250

It's worth trekking out here for the superb view of the Tallinn skyline, which featured in many old engravings of the city before it was usurped by Pirita's picture-postcard panorama. The old fortress walls and compact outline of Toompea are clearly visible, with Pikk Hermann soaring skywards on the right.

Lõime street, Tuulemaa, Ketraja (Spinners) streets
Kopli. *Map 1, C3, p250*

Here you will see examples of late-1940s and 1950s Stalinist architecture, inspired in equal measure by Italian palazzi and grandiose neoclassical architecture. If freshened up, these broad avenues – designed according to the belief that you could be anywhere in the Soviet Union and be equally at home in that great, forward-looking superstate – would be more than elegant.

Kneeling beauty
This decorative fountain was built in 1930 to prettify the park between the station and the Old Town.

Stroomi Beach
Bus 40 or 48 from the post office to Randla.
Map 1, D3, p250

Once something of a dump, the nearest beach to the town centre is now an attractive stretch with parkland and elegant globe lights just behind the shore. A bonfire is lit here at midsummer.

★ Rocca al Mare Open Air Museum
Vabaõhumuuseumi tee 12, **T** 654 9100, www.evm.ee. *May-Aug daily 1000-2000, buildings until 1800; Sep 1000-1800, buildings until 1700; Oct 1000-1800, buildings until 1600; Nov-Apr 1000-1700, buildings closed. 30 EEK in summer, 15 EEK in winter. Free with Tallinn Card. Bus 21 from Balti jaam. Map 1, E1, p250*

The 'Rock by the Sea', so named by Baltic German landlord Girard de Soucanton, who built his summer estate here in the 19th century, opened as a museum in the 1950s. The 18th-century farm buildings from across the country, including old thatched barn dwellings and wooden windmills were reassembled here in forests overlooking Kopli Bay and are equally beautiful in summer and winter. On weekends between May and August, folk dance groups give humorous displays at 1100. The not always elegant moves involve stepping over sticks and male dancers bumping each other's bottoms. The museum is also the site of low-key midsummer celebrations on 23 June. You can rent bicycles from the souvenir shop near the entrance (35 EEK per hr, 65 EEK for 2 hrs).

Loomaaed (Zoo)

Paldiski maantee 145, **T** 694 3300, www.tallinnzoo.ee. *50 EEK, students and pensioners 25 EEK, children 3 and over and pensioners over 70 4 EEK, family ticket 95 EEK. Free with Tallinn Card. Map 1, F1, p250*

Some of the cages for larger animals, such as the polar bear, are distressingly small, but this zoo is doing its bit for the extinct European mink. Home to the world's only artificially bred European mink population, the zoo has a breeding centre that seeks to reintroduce the mink on the islands of Hiiumaa and Saaremaa. It also has one of the world's best collections of rare species of goat and deer.

Lasnamäe

Many locals would rather you ignored this neighbourhood, but to be honest, that's impossible. For a start, this sprawling, 30 km² conglomeration of tower blocks, plonked on a limestone plateau east of Tallinn, is huge. It is also home to nearly a third of the city's population. Built for workers from the Soviet Union to take up jobs at factories and industrial plants producing goods occupied Estonia didn't even need (about 200,000 workers were settled in Tallinn, more than the city's entire population in 1945), it is also home to many Estonians, among them artists. Unsurprisingly, it is the cheapest place to live in Tallinn.

The newest of three estates hastily built on the three hills outside the city centre, Lasnamäe was started in 1977 and never finished – the tram line that was to connect it to the town centre, for example, was never built. Seen from the air, especially if it's cloaked in fresh snow, Lasnamäe has a weird, almost extraterrestrial beauty, but down on the ground it has a grittier look, due in part to the absence of greenery. Ironically, this neighbourhood is a stone's throw from an ancient Estonian settlement, the Iru hill fort, built in the seventh century and burnt down by rampaging Russians two centuries later.

Ask locals for a tour of Lasnamäe and they will probably think you are being sarcastic. One reluctant inhabitant said she did not feel particularly safe living here, especially at night (heroin is a problem), but added that things are getting better. Carefully tended flower beds go some way to breaking up the grey monotony and the infrastructure is improving, with larger and better shops opening; the local pizza parlour has a wood-fired oven, an authentic touch unimaginable in the Brezhnev years. Some privately owned blocks are undergoing facelifts thanks to the formation of residents' committees. The only fear is that if the powers that be fail to make the place more people-friendly, Estonians will make it their mission to move out, leaving a 'Russian ghetto' behind.

◉ Sights

Jüriöö Park (St George's Night Park)
Near the Hotel Susi (Peterburi tee 4). Map 1, F9, p251

The memorial commemorates the St George's Night uprising in 1343, when Estonian peasants were defeated by the German-Danish feudal lords. There are plans to erect a lighthouse in the park.

Nõmme

This garden suburb covers an even bigger area than Lasnamäe, spreading south along the highway to Pärnu, but it's home to just 11% of the city's population (40,000), and a paradise for anyone seeking a spot of peace and quiet. Villas are tucked away in pine forests (Nõmme means 'heath') and sprawling gardens ensure everyone privacy. The suburb developed after the opening of the local railroad station in 1872, as the local Baltic-German landlord, Nikolai von Glehn, sold land to the richer inhabitants of Tallinn, who built summer cottages here; it became a town in 1926. Permanent residences sprang up in the 1930s, when it was seen as a highly desirable place to live, and you can still see traces of Functionalist and art deco architecture amid the pines. Unsurprisingly, many of the residents were deported by the Soviets for being 'bourgeois'.

▸▸ *See Sleeping p135, Eating and drinking p159, Bars and clubs p173*

Getting there: Bus 36 from Viru väljak or electric train from Balti jaam.

 Sights

Nõmme Museum

Jaama 18, **T** 670 0202. *Tue-Fri 1000-1700, Sat 1000-1600. 10 EEK, free with Tallinn Card. Map 1, H3, p250*

Housed in the old railway station, this low-tech museum relates the history of the town. Some explanations in English.

Kristjan Raud Museum

Raua 8, **T** 670 0023, www.ekm.ee. *Thu-Sat 1000-1700; closed in Jul.* **T** *670 0023 for tours. Free. Map 1, H3, p250*

▶ Poetry of the tower blocks

Although Lasnamäe is the largest of Tallinn's Soviet housing estates, its alienating atmosphere is shared by its smaller siblings. The Estonian writer Mati Unt's modernist novel *The Autumn Ball* is set in Mustamäe (near Nõmme), where the main protagonist is described as "sharing his building with several hundred other people". The book captures the Soviet-era feel of anonymous prefabs where lifts howled past people's doors and the "air smelled of mouse droppings and foodstuffs", where every flat looked the same and people hopelessly scoured name plates trying to remember a home once visited when drunk. Still, one of the characters concedes that the "high-rise neighbourhood" has its "mood and secrets", and he is happy to watch "the awaking and dying of the play of shadows on the crude walls of the prefabricated sections". In Unt's fanciful short story *Love in Mustamäe*, a couple who never meet fall in love by looking at each other through the windows of their respective tower blocks; the woman even gets pregnant as a result. Former president Lennart Meri also writes about Mustamäe in his book *Silvery White* (1976). Referring to a schoolteacher's discovery of 4000-year-old arrowheads in the neighbourhood, he concludes: "There had been something there before, although that seemed hard to believe looking out of the window."

Much more interesting than the above, this exhibition devoted to Kristjan Raud (1865-1943), the illustrator of the national epic, *Kalevipoeg*, is found in the artist's green-painted 1920s wooden house. His chunky, symbolist-influenced works are the main draw.

Von Glehn's Castle and Park
Vana-Mustamäe 48. *Map 1, H1, p250*

Built in 1886 by the area's landlord, the castle is more of a modest folly. The park, which is essentially a forest, is a wonderfully remote place to roam. There are odd statues lurking in the grounds, including a stone crocodile and a peculiar-looking Kalevipoeg.

West of Tallinn 95

Singing sands, gentle cliffs, a waterfall and the ruins of a Soviet military base.

Viimsi and the islands 97

Coastal views, a war museum and as much unspoilt woodland as you can handle.

Lahemaa 100

Hoary forests, country mansions, fishing shacks and ancient graves in the Land of Bays.

Haapsalu 105

This sleepy spa town, crowned with spooky castle ruins, was once frequented by the stars and tsars of imperial Russia.

Pärnu 110

The country's summer capital thrives in the heat, when high culture and club culture come together on its white sands.

Tartu 117

The birthplace of Estonian nationalism has museums aplenty, a lively student nightlife and a beguiling bohemian edge.

West of Tallinn

The coast west of the capital is dotted with coves, sandy beaches and pine forests. Lured by the slogan "Buy a house for the price of a flat", many Tallinners are moving to the area's spreading suburbs. Beyond, 50 km from Tallinn, lies Paldiski, a bizarre blend of natural beauty and degenerating tower blocks, once home to the Soviet navy's nuclear-submarine training base. Retreating troops vandalized the military installations in the mid-1990s, and this shell of a town served as the grim backdrop for Lukas Moodysson's harrowing film Lilja 4-Ever *(2003), about a Russian girl tricked into prostitution. Close to the capital is tranquil Lohusalu, a pine-coated peninsula sprinkled with summer cottages and small beaches to which Tallinners flock in summer.*

▸▸ *See Eating and drinking p159*

◉ Sights

Kakumäe Beach
Bus 21b from Balti jaam to Kammelja. Map 4, p256

Located just before Tabasalu and west of Rocca al Mare, this is a well-tended beach in a pretty village of modest cottages and immodest modern villas surrounded by high fences.

Holocaust Memorial
Just beyond Klooga. *Bus 12, 107, 108, 109, 110, 126, 136, 147, 156, 157 or 241 from Balti jaam to Klooga. Map 4, p256*

From Tallinn, take a left turn after the town of Klooga, following the 'Holokausti' signs. A small road leads to an eerily silent clearing in the pine forest, with a grey stone memorial commemorating the spot where 2000 Jews, many transported here from Russia, were massacred by retreating Nazi troops on 19 September 1944.

Türisalu
25 km from Tallinn, just past Väna Jõesuu. *Map 4, p256*

The Russian version of *Hamlet* was filmed here, and the observation platform offers an uplifting view over gentle white cliffs and the bay and beaches below.

Lohusalu
Map 4, p256

You need a bit of imagination to hear the voices of the beach at romantic Laulasmaa ('Singing Sands'). According to local lore, it whistles under your feet when it has been baked by hot sun following a rainfall. At the peninsula's northern tip is the old fishing village of Lohusalu, with a modern marina and a pub.

Paldiski
Buses 157 and 241 from Balti jaam; electric train from Balti jaam. Map 4, p256

This sprawling town, 52 km from Tallinn, was the site of the Soviet Union's nuclear-submarine training base and was out of bounds for 50 years. It was the first and last place in Estonia to witness a Soviet military presence.

If you've never visited a Soviet town, the shoddiness of the lumpen prefabricated housing and the crumbling hulk of the submarine training school are depressing. Eastern Europe veterans, however, will be heartened by the absence of aimless, angry young men on the streets, the beautifully kept flowerbeds and trim patches of greenery all over town, and the children running happily in the playgrounds.

Pakri Peninsula
Peetri tee. *Map 4, p256*

Paldiski's pretty wooden train station recalls the days when it was a fashionable resort favoured by artists – hard to believe until you reach Pakri Peninsula, 3 km west of the town centre, towards the lighthouse. The flora and fauna in this long untouched area are flourishing, with butterflies breezing around wild flowers, ducks bobbing in the sea below and sea birds wheeling overhead. It's a wonderfully windswept spot for a walk – but stick to the paths, because the cliffs are dangerously crumbly.

Viimsi and the islands

It's worth heading to Viimsi, just beyond Pirita, for the continuing beauty of the coastal road and the dwindling silhouette of Tallinn, with smooth grey boulders scattered in the foreground. Viimsi is developing into a mini resort, with a growing number of hotels for those who prefer a bit of peace and quiet, as well as a couple of museums. Visit the old fishermen's island of Aegna, favoured by party bureaucrats in the Soviet era, or the peaceful, unspoilt and more interesting Naissaar ('Women's Island'). About an hour by ferry from the mainland, it is the most accessible of the Estonian islands. Its name dates from the 11th century, when it was reputedly the haunt of delectable damsels. Nowadays, you'll find hardly any women – or men – there, just beautiful beaches and forests. Although it's been a nature reserve since 1995, the island's primary role for centuries was a military one, and traces of the Tsarist and Soviet armies' dubious legacy can still be seen.

▶▶ *See Sleeping p136, Eating and drinking p159*

Bus 114 to Viimsi from Balti jaam.

◉ Sights

Laidoneri Muuseum
(General Laidoner's State War Museum)

Mõisa tee 1, Viimsi, **T** 60 91443, www.laidoner.ee. *Wed-Sat 1100-1700. Map 4, p256*

A museum devoted to Estonia's super trooper, General Johan Laidoner. Born in Viimsi in 1884, he was commander-in-chief during the Independence War, when the fledgling republic had to fend off the German Landeswehr and the Red Army; the Estonians were assisted by a British squadron, which succeeded in immobilizing the Bolshevik navy. The museum is housed in the pink Viimsi manor, which Laidoner received in recognition of his wartime services; sadly, during the Second World War, he was deported to the Soviet Union in 1940, dying in prison in 1953. As a final insult, his home was used by the radio intelligence centre of the Soviet navy.

Naissaar

Monica ferry, **T** 1185, www.saartereisid.ee. *Boats depart from Pirita; check the website for schedules. There are no boats in autumn or winter. The round trip costs 180 EEK, plus 200 EEK for a bike; family ticket 360 EEK, children under 7 free. Pick up an invaluable map (50 EEK) at the Nature Park Centre, up the hill from the port. Take mosquito repellent, water and a packed lunch. Map 4, p256*

Marked trails will take you to the main sights, but the joy of this car-free island lies in what you'll see while hiking or cycling along its paths and tracks: mushrooms the size of dinner plates; sea eagles soaring over pines; wild raspberries, blueberries and bilberries begging to be picked; acid-yellow butterflies and crickets hopping through the long grass. You can see Tallinn in the distance but this place is a world away. As it's fairly small – just 18.6 sq km – Naissaar is best done as a day trip, as ferries are infrequent and facilities extremely basic, but overnight camping or guesthouse accommodation can be arranged.

▸▸ *See also Tours, p29*

Walks on Naissaar

There are three marked trails on Naissaar: the **military trail**, around the north of the island (red); the southern **historical trail** (blue); and the central **nature trail** (green). Each is about 10 km long. Try to visit the southwest coast as well, for a sense of utter solitude and for the mines at Mädasadam. At several points, you'll cross a narrow-gauge railway, built by Tsarist troops in the run-up to the First World War.

The **military trail** takes in the octagonal lighthouse at Virby, almost at the tip of the island, and a Tsarist bunker and gun emplacement. The **historical trail** is the most interesting, leading you to the graves of British seamen involved in blockades of Tallinn during the Russian-Swedish War of 1808-09 and the Crimean War, a ramshackle but strangely moving wooden church, several secluded beaches, Peter the Great-era fortifications and the eerie mine-storage facility (see below). The **nature trail**'s highlights are the east coast's rolling seafront dunes; a deciduous forest to which, according to legend, the king of Denmark exiled a wayward daughter; and the peat bogs of Kunila and Kullkrooni.

A word of warning: despite extensive de-mining operations in the late 1990s, there are still live explosives from military munitions dumps scattered through the forests. The island is perfectly safe, but watch your step off the trails, and don't light a campfire outside a designated site.

Miinilaod (Mine Warehouses)

Covering 20 ha at the heart of Naissaar, this secret mine factory once supplied sea mines to the whole of the Soviet Union, and was the main reason the island was off limits to civilians throughout the occupation. Today, you can wander the site at will: it's an eerie, overgrown site. When the Russians left they made the mines safe at Mädasadam, on the west coast, a bizarre spot where rusting canisters are piled up like boulders or stranded on the shoreline.

Aegna and Prangli islands
Map 4, p256

Smaller, but no less perfectly formed, are Aegna and Prangli islands. Aegna, a favourite of native Tallinners, has a sandy beach and is fun for mushrooming and berry-picking. Take your own refreshments. Boats leave from Pirita harbour and are fairly regular. Prangli's main assets are its secluded bays and beaches. It's reached from Leppneeme Harbour, **T** 609 1319, east of Tallinn: there are two ferries a day (less in winter). Take bus 11 from Tallinn's Balti jaam.

Lahemaa

The Land of Bays is made up of four peninsulas jutting out into the Gulf of Finland, with numerous islands and islets off its shores. Estonia's largest national park has the country's most enchanting country manor at its heart, while well-marked nature trails and specialist tour guides can satisfy your curiosity about anything from beavers, bears and bogs to folk dances and fisheries. The landscape is rich and varied, with limestone cliffs, coastal lakes, ancient forests and a coastline dotted with erratic boulders dragged across by ice sheets from Scandinavia (although folklore claims they were hurled by mighty Kalevipoeg). Riding through Lahemaa, you will pass hoary old fir trees, birches, oaks and open, luminous green fields; the smell of pine can be overwhelming.

▸▸ *See Sleeping p136, Eating and drinking p160*

Getting there: it takes about an hour by bus from Tallinn's bus station. A local bus from Viitna takes you to Palmse Visitor Centre, Võsu and Käsmu (Mon-Wed, Fri and Sun only, leaving Viitna at 1250). If you are driving, be warned that signposting is poor, roads are narrow and turns are often indicated at the last minute. To reach Lahemaa from Tallinn, take the E20 via Peterburi tee, which takes you past Lasnamäe, then leave the main road at Viitna, 50 km from Tallinn. The visitor centre is at Palmse Manor. Freelance guides must be booked in advance; recommendations from the visitor centre.

Jõelähtme

Information centre **T** 60 33097, margit.partel@mail.ee. *1 May-1 Oct Mon-Fri 0900-1700; other times open on request. 10 EEK. Buses 89, 102, 104, 106, 129, 134, 143, 150-155, 717, on the right of the motorway. Map 4, p256*

En route to Lahemaa, you pass a collection of extraordinary stone-cist graves, circled by a limestone wall, which date back as far as 700 BC. Objects found during excavation – animal bones, unburnt human bones and a few bronze items – are similar to those discovered in Jutland, Denmark. There's a small museum and information centre on the spot.

Palmse Manor

Palmse, **T** 32 40070. *Map 4, p256*

With its wooded park, orchards and serene swan lake, 18th-century Palmse Manor is one of the most beautiful and best-restored estates in the Baltic countries. The cream-and-yellow main building, started in 1698 and rebuilt in the 1880s, has a neoclassical façade with traces of baroque, and is much less pompous than many Baltic German manor houses. The estate belonged to the von der Pahlen family, but was expropriated by the Estonian government in the 1920s. The old distillery has been turned into a hotel and restaurant, while the bathhouse has become a sublimely romantic café.

Lahemaa Visitor Centre

Palmse Manor, **T** 32 95555, info@lahemaa.ee. *May-Aug daily 0900-1900; Sep 0900-1700; Oct-Apr Mon-Fri 0900-1700. Map 4, p256*

Housed in the manor's former stables, this visitor centre has a small auditorium where you can watch a beautifully shot documentary that offers an excellent introduction to the park's history and to what lives, grows, flies and swims here. The country's sole surviving freshwater pearl mussels are in Lahemaa; moose may be spotted after sunset, and the islets are perfect breeding habitats for sea birds. This is also the place to pick up maps and explanatory pamphlets.

Sagadi Manor

Sagadi (8 km northeast of Palmse via Oandu), **T** 32 58888, www.rmk.ee/metsamuseum. *Forest and manor daily May-Oct 1000-1800. Map 4, p256*

Long, low and mulberry-coloured, the manor house is less impressive than Palmse, but has similarly tranquil grounds. In one of its outbuildings, you'll find the **Forest Museum**, which describes the country's forests, the use of the forest and hunting. Most information is available in English.

Fishermen's shacks, Lahemaa
The Land of Bays is stunning year-round.

Walks around Lahemaa
Map 4, p256

Nearby Oandu is the start point for two of Lahemaa's best wildlife walks: on the 4.7-km **Oandu Forest Nature Trail**, you may find at least traces of the presence of brown bears, moose, wild boars and lynxes; while on the 1-km **Beaver Trail**, you'll see dams and, if you're lucky, the reclusive beast itself. There are information boards in English. Don't leave valuables in the car.

Altja
5 km from Sagadi. *Map 4, p256*

This is a typical coastal fishermen's village, with grey thatched barn dwellings and a popular, if touristy, tavern (see Eating, p160).

Käsmu
From Altija, take the coastal road via Vergi and the Võsu holiday village. Map 4, p256

Situated on Käsmu Bay and first mentioned in 1453, Lahemaa's loveliest village was, according to legend, founded by a captain named Kaspar, who survived a shipwreck and built a chapel here. Legend also tells us that Gustav Adolf II of Sweden, the country's most revered monarch, wound up here after a rough sea voyage and etched his name on a stone at Palganamee. Traditionally a shipbuilding village, its chief draws are the delightful wooden seaside cottages and villas. Käsmu is a good base from which to explore the peninsula, using either a 11-km hiking trail or a 14-km bicycle route.

Käsmu Museum
Käsmu, **T** 32 38136. *Daily 1000-1800 (sometimes longer hours). Donations (about 10 EEK). Map 4, p256*

This seafront museum in a former border guard's house has a rambling collection of lanterns, fishing nets, ropes, coloured bottles, models of boats and souvenirs from Pisa, Genoa, Sunderland, Zeebrugge and Canada. One book on display conveys the romance of sea tales (the author describes how, as a boy, he stayed up late listening to his father's stories, desperately hoping his mother would not notice that he was still awake).

Muuksi Linnamägi
Map 4, p256

Muuksi is home to the country's biggest stone-cist cemetery, which some say dates back to 2600 BC. At Linnamägi (meaning 'site of an ancient fortified stronghold'), turn right through fields of wild flowers and climb a flight of stone steps up to a small hill.

Viinistu Kunstimuuseum (Viinistu Art Museum)
Viinistu, **T** 51 57270, www.viinistukunst.ee. *Jul-Aug daily 1100-1800; Sep-May Wed-Sun 1100-1800. 10 EEK. Buses 89, 129, 139, 150-155, 717. Map 4, p256*

This fascinating museum, on the northernmost tip of the Viinistu Peninsula, was founded by Jaan Manitski, a local businessman whose family fled to Sweden during the Second World War. Manitski became financial advisor to ABBA and returned to Estonia after the restoration of its independence. Inside, you can admire his private art collection, which includes works by 19th-century Baltic German painters and the creations of leading contemporary Estonian artists. It's a good overview of Estonian art and a must for art-lovers. Manitski has also opened an airy, calm seafront hotel next door.

Haapsalu

The resort of Haapsalu, a slightly faded but atmospheric town of wooden villas with lacy carved trimmings, rose to fame with the discovery of curative mud in the early 19th century. The city was so popular with the Tsars that a 216-m train platform was built to welcome Russia's royals. Tchaikovsky also favoured this peaceful place and a memorial bench looking out to sea remembers his presence. An important ecclesiastical stronghold in the 13th century, Haapsalu remained the seat of power for the Saare-Lääne bishopric until it fell to the Swedes during the Livonian War. During the Northern War, the castle was reduced to ruins, which were transformed into a peaceful park in the 19th century. Many of the Swedes who settled here fled across the Baltic to Sweden during the Second World War. The Cathedral of St Nicholas was reopened for services in 1990, having narrowly escaped being turned into a swimming pool by the Soviets.
▸▸ *See Sleeping p137, Eating and drinking p162*

Sights

Castle ruins
Lossi plats. *Map 4, p256*

The rough stone ruins of the medieval fortress, with red-tiled roofs and skeletal window silhouettes framing patches of sky, are set in parkland and provide the backdrop for August's White Lady Days (Valge Daami Päevad), when a ghostly white apparition can be seen in the window of the cathedral's baptismal chapel at full moon. According to legend, this is the ghost of a young woman beloved by a canon who smuggled her into the religious community. When discovered, she was walled up and left to die; the canon was imprisoned and starved to death. Every year, an open-air play re-enacts this sorry tale. If you get a kick out of weapons, pop into the **Museum and Watchtower of the Episcopal Castle** (*May-Sep Tue-Sun 1000-1800, 10 EEK for watchtower, 15 EEK for castle, children half price*), where the collection includes a dolomite mould for casting cannonballs. Otherwise, head straight for the watchtower and its wide-angle views of land and sea. There's a **tourist information** kiosk just outside the castle by the car park.

Cathedral of St Nicholas
Nigula 49, **T** 47 96658. *Tue-Fri 1000-1400, service Sun 1200. Map 4, p256*

Rebuilt in the 19th century, then left to decay for decades after the Second World War, St Nicholas celebrated its first religious service in the nascent Estonia in 1990. Stark and white inside, it's a calm, contemplative space with an altar donated by a local doctor whose mother was deported to, and died in, Siberia. In the circular baptismal chapel, completed in the 15th century, you can see a modest box containing Siberian earth, a memorial to Estonian mothers killed during the Soviet occupation.

Läänemaa Muuseum

Kooli 2, **T** 47 37065, www.muuseum.haapsalu.ee. *Wed-Sun 1000-1800. 15 EEK. Map 4, p256*

Visiting local history museums in Estonia can be a poignant experience, as you realize what the place looked like before the Soviet planners got their teeth into it. Here you'll find photographs of elegant pre-war Haapsalu, when a Mickey Mouse statue graced the promenade, and an engaging assortment of exhibits from earlier days, including a reconstructed peasant dwelling and a coin from the time of Richard the Lionheart.

Kuursaal

Promenaadi 1, **T** 47 35505, www.kuursaal.ee. *May-Sep daily 1000-0200. Map 4, p256*

On first glance, this wondrous wooden entertainment hall appears to be floating in the sea. A warehouse during the Soviet era, it has been renovated and turned into a restaurant and concert venue.

Seaside walk and Tchaikovsky's Bench
Map 4, p256

Follow the seaside walk north from the Kuursaal, past reeds, gliding swans and diving ducks, and you will come to a stone bench beside a flowerbed, erected in 1940 in honour of Tchaikovsky, who summered here in 1867. A few bars of the composer's *Sixth Symphony* are inscribed onto the seat. Press a button and the bench blasts out Tchaikovsky's most popular pieces, including *Swan Lake*. Tacky, but strangely satisfying.

Estonian Railway Museum

Raudtee 2, **T** 47 34574, www.jaam.ee. *Thu-Sun 1000-1800.*
15 EEK. Map 4, p256

Haapsalu's long, low-slung railway station is a wonderfully
elaborate cream-and-brown wooden building that has featured in
a host of films. Original tiles and mosaics have been preserved in
the entrance hall, giving an atmospheric, *Anna Karenina* feel. In
fact, the only thing that's missing is a train service: the Haapsalu
line was closed in 1995 and the station is used for buses instead.
Around the back, which is still faded and peeling, you can visit that
216-m railway platform, one of imperial Russia's longest (the idea
was that the Tsar and his retinue would not be inconvenienced by
the weather), and run the rule over several old locomotives.

Vormsi Island

*A 45-minute ferry trip (**T** 47 32308) from Rohuküla Harbour,
10 km west of Haapsalu. Schedule changes seasonally; see
www.laevakompanii.ee for details. 30 EEK return, 110 EEK cars
return, concessions available.*

This gently undulating island, coated with wooded meadows,
forest and junipers, is home to just 340 people. It used to be a little
more crowded. The substantial Swedish community fled before
the Soviet takeover in 1944, although their legacy can be felt in the
village names and the elaborate porches of the villas and cottages.
Hullo, in the centre, has an old forest cemetery with Swedish-style
circular crosses, some crumbling, others half swallowed by the
earth. The loveliest spot is the Rumpo Peninsula, where a remote
path takes you seawards through a nature reserve of wild flowers,
thistles and tufty junipers, alive with butterflies and dragonflies.
For bike rental on Vormsi, **T** 051 78722.

▶ Bear necessities

Ask the staff at Lahemaa's information centre where to spot a bear and they will advise you to go to a zoo. Although a handful of Estonia's 600 brown bears live in Lahemaa, they hibernate from November to March, and the closest most of us are likely to get to glimpsing one is – gulp – at mealtimes. Bear is regarded as a speciality in some Estonian restaurants (not, however, in Lahemaa). There is a long tradition of bear-hunting in Estonia (the country's first feature film was *Bear Hunt in Pärnu*), and the issue proved thorny during negotiations with the anti-hunting European Union. Estonia won the day by arguing that legal culls are sometimes necessary to protect other species, and that farmers are best placed to keep an eye on the size of the bear population. In recent years, one young bear wandered into Tallinn and tried to clamber into an apartment. It was tranquillized and returned to the forest. About 50 bears a year can be legally killed by licensed hunters; the bear meat served in restaurants comes from these culls. The museum at Sagadi Manor has a section on hunting, see p102.

Matsalu Nature Reserve

Information Centre, Penijõe Manor House, Penijõe, near Lihula, **T** 47 24236, www.hot.ee/matsalu. *Map 4, p256*

The remote coastal region of Matsalu, 130 km southwest of Tallinn, is the largest nesting place for migrant sea birds in the Baltic region and a bird sanctuary of international importance. There are five observation towers, including the Haeska tower, which Finnish ornithologists say is one of the best in northern Europe. The best time to visit is in April and May (serious birdwatchers should telephone in advance to make sure the towers are open). Whether or not you spot birds, it's worth coming here for the wild, windswept terrain, with its islets, forests, coastal meadows, juniper pastures and dreamy sea views. The Kasari flood plain is one of Europe's largest surviving open alluvial meadows. Matsalu is also home to ancient burial mounds, tangy old fishing villages and Estonia's largest snail. Hikers should pick up the *Hiking Around Matsalu* brochure from the information centre. For further information about birds, visit the Estonian Ornithological Society's website, www.eoy.ee.

Pärnu

Estonia's self-styled summer capital is famous for its long strand of white sand and the vigour of its cultural and social life in high season, as sun-deprived Estonians, worn down by months of long, dark nights, hit the beach and shed much of their winter reserve. Once a member of the Hanseatic League, Pärnu has been a holiday resort since 1838, with bracing mud baths one of its main attractions; although it was described as "almost Riviera-dazzling" by a pre-war English writer, it's less polished and less narcissistic than that suggests. Space-obsessed Estonians say the beach is too crowded in summer, but crowded is a relative term, and it's rarely unbearable.

The town centre, spread around the main street, Rüütli, has a delightfully dozy feel, while parkland and fragrant pine woods lie between town and sea. When you're bored of the beach, you can spend hours wandering aimlessly along streets lined with functionalist villas, fairy-tale wooden houses and sprawling private gardens filled with lilac and apple trees. Behind this idyllic façade lies a cutting-edge core, with challenging contemporary art shows, good theatre and world-class concerts at the sparkling steel and glass concert hall.

▸▸ *See Sleeping p138, Eating and drinking p160, Bars and clubs p173*

! The information centre provides a free brochure called *Discovering Historical Pärnu*, with a handy map.

> ### Body language, Estonian style

Estonians, on the whole, are not physically very demonstrative. Kissing someone on the cheek by way of greeting may be considered rather forward and invasive by more old-fashioned people. Traditionally you should say hello and goodbye with a handshake (but never shake hands across a threshold; you should both be inside or outside). When an Estonian wants to express that little bit more warmth and appreciation, they have a funny habit of doing a bob. It's not exactly a bow or curtsey; it's more subtle than that. Some foreigners think it means they are being treated with excessive deference, but it just means the person enjoyed meeting you. So, you can bob but you can't kiss. Younger people tend to be freer and more open in spirit.

◉ Sights

Pärnu Beach

Pärnu's pride and joy is its long, soft, sandy beach, dotted with brightly painted benches and swings, volleyball nets and primitive changing kiosks covered with cosmetics ads. The Sunset Club, housed in the functionalist beach café, with its mushroom-shaped terrace and seafront decking area, is the main venue for parties.

Cars must be left several streets back (parking 25 EEK for two hours, 50 EEK for a day). There are plenty of kiosks selling snacks and suncream behind the beach, where you can stroll through pine woods or hire bicycles (**T** 50 28269), in-line skates or motorized scooters (**T** 50 18121/56 457 732). One kiosk has internet access (40 EEK per hour).

Pärnu Mudaravila (mud baths)

Ranna puiestee 1, **T** 44 25523 (24 hours), www.mudaravila.ee.
Reservations essential; 150 EEK for a mud bath, cash only. Map 4, p257

If a mud bath is a must, the best place to try it is this neoclassical
cream-and-pink confection, constructed in 1927. Inside, uniformed
staff walk briskly through the echoing, high-ceilinged corridors,
while ailing patients, as well as the simply curious, gaze at the
lemon-and-cream walls; the atmosphere is sober, the aroma
slightly chemical. The mud, which comes from Haapsalu, is used
to treat joint and spinal problems, radiculitis, cardiovascular
disorders, diseases of the locomotive system and the peripheral
nervous system, functional disorders of the nervous system and
even gynaecological diseases.

Rannahotell

Ranna puiestee 5. *Map 4, p257*

This ship-shaped structure, with circular windows, deck-like
railings and a curved section resembling a funnel, is one of the
purest and most beautiful Functionalist buildings in Europe. The
style, which followed the doctrine that form must be function-led,
was hugely popular in the 1920s and 1930s, when Pärnu was
developing at lightning pace, which explains the many flat-
topped, streamlined villas. The town architect at the time, Olav
Siinmaa, was an enthusiast; his own house (Rüütli 1a) is a weird
modernistic mix of no-frills surfaces and dizzyingly odd angles.

Kuursaal

Mere puiestee 22, **T** 44 20367, www.kuur.ee. *Sun-Thu 1200-0200,
Fri and Sat 1200-0400. Map 4, p257*

Built in 1880, this sprawling summer pavilion lacks the elegance of
its counterpart in Haapsalu, but it's a far livelier affair, with live

▶ Mud, sweat and tears

Taking to the mud can be something of a shock. First, it is not a very private experience. The rooms can take two people at once, and you may find yourself undressing in front of an apparently much less inhibited Finnish woman (or man, if you're in a room for men). Second, you do not lie in a bath of mud, but on a bed, with a wrap. Third, you probably won't be prepared for the heat. The mud is warmed to 42°C, and the first contact as you place your bottom on it makes you gasp for an escape. If you protest, you are kindly but firmly told that there is no turning back. Your body is then coated in hot, fudgy, slimy sludge, and you are wrapped in what feels uncomfortably like a body bag.

On no account should you put your arms inside the wrap; if you do, you will almost certainly develop an itchy nose, and unless you can say "Excuse me, but would you mind scratching my nose?" in Estonian or Finnish, nobody is going to help. After 15 minutes, when you have surrendered to the womb-like warmth and almost nodded off, you are briskly unwrapped and invited to shower. Try as you might, you cannot quite get rid of the slightly sulphurous, seaweedy stink. It is not for the claustrophobic and certainly not for anyone with a heart condition. If you have any doubts about your health, consult a doctor first. There are plenty in situ.

music and DJs in summer. The cavernous yet cosy interior is a bizarre mix of Black Forest hunting lodge and provincial discotheque, with a huge dancefloor at its back, while the vast terrace out back offers views of the bijou local song bowl, ringed with coloured bulbs.

Ammende's Villa
Mere puiestee 7. *Map 4, p257*

One of the finest examples of Art Nouveau in Estonia, this flamboyant blend of the Brussels style with a hint of Russian influence was completed by St Petersburg architects in 1905. It is now an upmarket hotel with a sprawling terrace and one of the best restaurants in town. It was built for merchant Hermann Ammende's daughter's wedding party.

Pärnu Uue Kunsti Muuseum (Museum of New Art)
Esplanaadi 10, **T** 44 30772, www.chaplin.ee. *Daily 0900-2100. Map 4, p257*

Housed in an ugly former Communist building a few streets north of the beach, this well-designed museum hosts excellent contemporary-art exhibitions, with a seasonally appropriate summer show on the loose theme of nudity. The work on display is mostly of international quality. The café's coffee is not up to much – bizarrely, you can take home bags of much better stuff – but it's a relaxing enough place to sit. There's a good bookshop (1100-1700) with tourist guides and maps as well as books on art. You can also access the internet here (15 EEK for 30 mins).

Pärnu Old Town
Map 4, p257

Little remains of the ramparts of this frequently besieged fortress town besides its **17th-century gatehouse**, with pretty orange and green doors. **Punane Torn** (Red Tower), at Hommiku 11, is one of the town's oldest buildings. A stolid, three-floor fortress tower dating from the 15th century, it's now, confusingly, white.

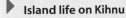

▶ Island life on Kihnu

The tiny island of Kihnu is just 40 km southwest of Pärnu, but it is a world unto itself, so much so that it was added to UNESCO's Intangible Heritage list in 2003. Here you can still see the distinctive *kala* bikes (scooters with large wooden fish boxes attached) bumping along dusty tracks, often driven by women wearing traditional brightly coloured striped skirts and headscarves. You can see women in folk costume tilling the fields, too. In fact, women seem to do most of the hard work on the island, their men content to fish – and drink like fish when there is nothing to catch. Most of the 500 or so islanders adhere to the Orthodox faith, having converted when Tsarist Russia offered land to those who adopted the religion. Just 7 km by 3.3 km, the island can easily be visited in a day. There's a modest local museum in the village of Linaküla, but the real pleasure here is wandering through the forests, picking wild strawberries as you go, and drifting along narrow roads past old-fashioned farmsteads. Sticklers for tradition should come here for St John's Night, which is celebrated in time-honoured fashion. Ferries leave from Munalaiu Port, 40 km from Pärnu (75 EEK for a return ticket), but the most exhilarating way to arrive is by fisherman's boat; contact the Kihnurand Travel Agency (**T** 044 69924, www.kihnu.ee/kihnurand.html) for more information.

Tallinn Gate
Kuninga 1. *Map 4, p257*

Erected in 1667 and rebuilt the following century, this gatehouse once marked the old route to Tallinn. Today, it's the unofficial gateway from the Old Town to the resort area. You can walk along the nearby moat, admiring the romantic rampart ruins and open-air amphitheatre, where concerts are held in summer.

Jekateriina Church (St Catherine's church)

Vee 16. *Daily 0900-1600. Map 4, p257*

The richest example of ecclesiastical baroque architecture in the country, this gaily painted green-and-yellow Orthodox church was built in the second half of the 18th century on the orders of Catherine the Great, who passed through Pärnu in 1764.

Eliisabeti Church (Elizabeth's church)

Nikolai 22, **T** 44 31381. *Jun-Aug daily 1200-1800, Sep-May Mon-Fri 1000-1400. Map 4, p257*

If nothing else, the architect of this ochre-tinted mid-18th-century church deserves credit for attempting to reconcile the wildly contrasting concepts of Lutheran and baroque; although unusually ornate by the standards of northern European Protestantism, it's still a long way from being excessive. Named after Empress Elizabeth of Russia, it has one of the best organs in Estonia and frequently hosts concerts. There's a bizarre rose window whose stained glass recalls the 'cheeses' used in Trivial Pursuit.

Pärnu Muuseum (Museum of Pärnu)

Rüütli 53, **T** 44 33231, www.pernau.ee. *Wed-Sun 1000-1800. 30 EEK. Map 4, p257*

Located in a dismal modern building enlivened a little by a symbol of a boat, this old-fashioned museum explores the history of the town from its origins in 9000 BC. No commentary in English. The museum is awaiting a move to new premises in a converted 19th-century granary on Aida, opposite the concert hall.

Kontserdimaja (Concert Hall)

Aida 4, **T** 44 55810, www.concert.ee. *Box office Mon-Fri 1200-1900, Sat 1000-1600, Sun 1 hr before concert.* Map 4, p257

Opened in 2002, this stunning steel-and-glass venue next to the river has state-of-the-art acoustics. As well as big-name pop, world music and classical concerts, it hosts free contemporary-art exhibitions showcasing local and international names. The galleries are spread over three floors, so you can admire the views as well as the art.

Lydia Koidula Memorial Museum

Jannseni 3, **T** 44 33313. *Wed-Sun 1000-1700. 15 EEK.* Map 4, p257

The dilapidated façade does not prepare you for the polished interiors of the house where one of Estonia's most significant poets was brought up. Visit the schoolroom, where Koidula's father, a leading figure in the country's National Awakening, founded the first Estonian newspaper (*Perno Postimees*) and taught Estonian to local fishermen's children. The family later moved to Tartu, and Koidula, having married a doctor from Riga, settled on Kronstadt, an island near St Petersburg, where she longed for her native land and died young of cancer, leaving two daughters and a nation forever in awe of her patriotic poetry.

Tartu

Ask Estonians if there is serious rivalry between Tallinn and Tartu and they will say: "It's a joke – sort of." The university town – birthplace of Estonia's National Awakening and of the first national song festival (1869), and rich in vaim *(spirit) – regards itself as intellectually superior to Tallinn, city of* võim *(power). The difference is captured in a play on words: Tallinn is the "pealinn" (capital, or head city); Tartu is "peagalinn" (the city with a head). Tartu people deride the capital as* hectic and money-obsessed; Tallinners concede that the inhabitants of Estonia's Oxbridge are educated, independent-minded guardians of that elusive thing, the 'Estonian spirit', but consider them just a tad slow and naïve. Ironically, almost everyone who's anyone in the big smoke is a Tartu graduate. The local tourist office calls Tartu 'a city of good thoughts', a slogan that, in true Tartu style, was chosen after a public competition. At first glance, this rambling former Hanseatic town, with a river lazily meandering through it, is underwhelming, and you need a little imagination to appreciate the spirit of the 'Athens of the North'. First mentioned in the 1030s, Tartu has lost its medieval looks thanks to fire, war and destruction, although many of its cool, pale façades date back to the 18th century, and the city was spruced up for the 25th International Hanseatic Days event in 2005. The best time to visit is during university term time, ideally during the Spring Days student festival, which winds up on 1 May with partying into the early hours.

▸▸ *See Sleeping p140, Eating and drinking p162, Bars and clubs p174, Festivals p185*

Getting there: Tartu is a 2½-hour bus ride from Tallinn. Buses leave roughly every half-hour and tickets cost 75-90 EEK. Tartu bus station, Turu 2, **T** 7 331 277.

Sights

Raekoja plats (Town Hall Square)
Map 4, p257

Most of this cobbled, pedestrianized ensemble is neoclassical in appearance, the result of the devastating fire of 1775, after which the crooked medieval streets were straightened up. The town hall has a few baroque flourishes; its carillon rings out a variety of tunes to suit the seasons and time of day, often ending with a lullaby (1200, 1800 and 2100). The **Kissing Students Fountain** is a delightfully upbeat representation of sophomores snogging under a dripping umbrella.

Tartu Art Museum

Raekoja plats 18, **T** 7 441 080, www.tartmus.ee. *Wed-Sun 1100-1800. 10 EEK, concessions 5 EEK, Fri free. Map 4, p257*

The spectacularly lopsided house, which belonged to the wife of Russian field marshal Michael Andreas Barclay de Tolly (1761-1818), is a splendid setting for excellent temporary exhibitions, including retrospectives of Estonian art. Its wonky look is due to the lowering of the water level.

Slow Death

Map 4, p257

This staggeringly steep path behind Raekoja plats leads to Toomemägi (Dome Hill), once part of the city's fortification system, but transformed into parkland two centuries ago. Both are dotted with monuments to leading cultural and academic figures. The statue of a young man clutching a staff is a tribute to Kristjan Jaak Peterson (1801-1822), the first poet to write in Estonian, who died of tuberculosis; Estonia's Language Day (14 March) marks his birthday. The seated, reflective figure is Karl Ernst von Baer (1792-1876), founder of embryology.

! One of Tartu's good ideas was to hold a sculpture competition to design road blocks. The resulting turtles and other figures are certainly more aesthetic than your average bollard – and more practical, too, since you can actually sit on them.

Cathedral ruins and around
Map 4, p257

Partially restored, these soaring red-brick and ruins, with spectacular cross-ribbed vaults, are all that remains of the St Peter and St Paul Cathedral, completed in the 15th century and destroyed in the Livonian War. Nearby is Tartu's most impressive viewing platform. Cross **Angel's Bridge**, where you can pause to enjoy views of green and leafy Tartu, as well as some houses in a sorry state of disrepair (some owned by Estonian émigrés who cannot be traced, a real dilemma for the city), then make for the **Old Observatory**, one of Europe's most prestigious at the turn of the past century. In 1967, the observatory was moved to a more remote location to prevent the bright city lights obscuring interplanetary vision.

Estonian National Museum
Kuperjanovi 9, **T** 7 421 311, www.erm.ee. *Wed-Sun 1100-1800, 12 EEK (20 EEK for all exhibitions, temporary and permanent), concessions 8 EEK (14 EEK), Fri free. Map 4, p257*

A fascinating museum dedicated to the folklore collector, Jakob Hurt. It presents Estonian history according to the various ethnic groups that have shaped it, among them the Swedes and the Baltic Germans.

The Citizen's Museum
Jaani 16, **T** 7 361 545. *Apr-Sep Wed-Sun 1000-1500, Oct-Mar Wed-Sun 1100-1500. 8 EEK, concessions 5 EEK, guided tour in English 120 EEK. Map 4, p257*

This is an evocative re-creation of the home of a middle-class citizen in the 19th century; look out for the rather frightening wooden implement used to mash lumps out of porridge.

Jaani Kirik (St John's Church)

Lutsu 16-3. *Map 4, p257*

This is one of the finest examples of brick Gothic architecture in northern Europe. The use of such brick was common in southern Estonia, where limestone is in shorter supply than it is up north. Delicately decorated with tiny and life-size terracotta figures – the largest such collection in Northern Europe – the church dates back to the 14th century. It was threatened with demolition during the Soviet occupation; an emotional ceremony to mark its restoration was held in 2005.

River Emajõgi

From Raekoja plats, head east across Vabaduse puiestee. *Map 4, p257*

The once-loved bridge was bombed by the Soviets during the Second World War and replaced by one that does its best to be unlovable. Cross it fast and enjoy a riverside stroll along a willow-lined path. The statue of Kalevipoeg, removed by the Soviets but replaced on Midsummer's Eve 2003, stands next to his creator, Kreutzwald. There are plans to rebuild the original 18th-century bridge in all its glory.

From the port (Soola 5, **T** 7 340 066, www.transcom.ee/tartusadam), you can take one-hour cruises down the Emajõgi (*May-Sep, departures 1100, 1300, 1500 and 1700; 50 EEK*), or, if you have time, to Värska (*120 EEK*), on the shores of Lake Peipsi, the vast lake that divides Estonia from Russia.

Estonian Literary Museum
Vanaemuise 42, **T** 7 377 700. *Mon-Thu 0900-1700, Fri to 1630. Map 4, p257*

Around 15 minutes southwest of the Town Hall on foot, this museum houses the all-important Estonian folk poetry and folklore collection. If you want help in English, give ample warning of your visit. The pale-blue 'small' Vanemuine Theatre (Vanemuise), once known as the German theatre, has a beautiful Jugendstil façade.

Old KGB Cells
Riia 15b, **T** 7 461 717. *Tue-Sat 1100-1600. 5 EEK, concessions 3 EEK, tour in English 80 EEK. Map 4, p257*

On the corner of Riia and Pepleri streets, the former South Estonian headquarters of the NKVD/KGB now pays tribute to the anti-Soviet resistance movement, which could not be quashed despite deportation and repression. About 20,000 Estonians, 2.5% of the population, were deported in March 1949 alone; in total 122,000 people were persecuted, more than 30,000 of whom perished. You can visit the basement cells, several of which contain an exhibition on Soviet crimes. Objects from the Gulag hard-labour camps (by 1946, 6% of the inhabitants were from the Baltic states) are also on display.

The hotel business is booming in Tallinn, with a welcome expansion in the range of accommodation available. In the 1990s, as foreign investment flowed in, business-oriented hotels sprang up south of the Old Town, with cheaper accommodation near the port catering mainly to Finnish tourists. Recently, attractive boutique hotels have begun to appear in the Old Town, alongside spas catering primarily to Scandinavians. Prices are low by European standards, especially outside Tallinn, and most hotels offer free extra beds to children (although age limits vary). A better choice of furnishings means that the newest hotels are usually the most tasteful. Most hotels have rooms for the disabled and those with allergies, and dial-up, broadband or WiFi internet connections are available even in the smaller hotels. At the other extreme, the number of hostels is also growing, although more rooms are needed to cope with the peak season. Early reservation is essential, especially during the National Song Festival and around midsummer. Hotels are harder to fill in winter, so serious discounts are par for the course.

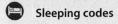

Sleeping codes

LL	4695 EEK and over	**D**	780-1160 EEK
L	3915-4670 EEK	**E**	550-780 EEK
AL	3130-3900 EEK	**F**	400-550 EEK
A	2350-3115 EEK	**G**	under 400 EEK
B	1565-2335 EEK	Prices are per night for a
C	1175-1550 EEK	double room in high season

Price (vertical label at left)

From summer 2006, look out for three new Old Town options:
Viru Inn, a hotel/restaurant in a merchant's house on Viru street;
Savoy Boutique Hotel, handily placed for the bars of Suur-Karja,
and **Telegraf**, another five-star offering from the people behind
the Three Sisters.

Toompea

Hotels and guesthouses
Note that the hotels listed below are situated at the foot of the hill
and not actually within the upper town itself.

A Meriton Grand Hotel Tallinn, Toompuiestee 27, **T** 667
7000, www.grandhotel.ee. *Map 1, D5, p250* A highly
professional four-star former Intourist hotel with a shiny lobby,
a glass lift and a fitness centre. Ridiculously perfect views of park
and castle from the cocktail bar and rooms on the upper floors
(ask for a room away from Toompuiestee if noise annoys). Rooms
are on the right side of bland, with beige furnishings and green
carpets. Free morning sauna. Children under 12 free.

Apartment stays and B&Bs

The apartment rental business is booming. Prices start at about 800 EEK per night for an Old Town apartment. The most established agency offering rooms in private homes is **Rasastra** (Mere puiestee 4, **T** 661 6291, www.bedbreakfast.ee).

The following companies rent apartments in the Old Town and Town Centre (Kesklinn): **Old Town Residence** (Pärnu maantee 10, **T** 640 5850, www.guesthouse.ee); **Kullassepa Residence** (Kullassepa 9/11, **T** 623 2055, mobile 5048 787); **Oldhouse Guesthouse** (see p130); **Romeo Family Hotel** (see p130); **Cassandra** (Tartu maantee 18, **T** 630 9820, www.cassandra-apartments.com); **Erel Group** (Tartu maantee 14, **T** 610 8780, www.erel.ee); **Ites Apartments**, Harju 6, **T** 631 0637, www.ites.ee..

C Nordic Hotel L'Ermitage, Toompuiestee 19, **T** 699 6400, **F** 699 6401, www.nordichotels.ee. *Map 1, D5, p250* This slickly run modern hotel opposite the parkland at the foot of Toompea has good-sized rooms, some with wrought-iron beds and all with architecture photographs on the walls. The colour scheme varies from floor to floor. Book the spacious purple Luxury Suite and you can breakfast on the balcony. Children under seven stay free in their parents' room.

C Unique-Stay, Paldiski maantee 3 and Toompuiestee 23, **T** 660 0700, **F** 661 6176, www.uniquestay.com. *Map 1, E5, p250* Opposite the Grand Hotel. The 11 Zen rooms are decidedly New Age, with aromatherapy, NASA-designed chairs and whirlpool baths. Arty photos lend a touch of gravitas. Free parking, free 24-hour internet access; under-12s free.

D Shnelli Hotel, Toompuiestee 37, **T** 631 0100, **F** 631 0101, www.gohotels.ee. *Map 1, D5, p250* Named after a city gardener, this is a large modern hotel next to the railway station. The rooms are plain, with wooden furniture and orange fabrics, and have a slightly anonymous feel. It's worth paying the extra 90 EEK for a view of Toompea.

Hostels

E Hostel Alur, Rannamäe tee 3, **T** 631 1531. *Map 1, C3, p252* Just across from Toompea, this clean and comfortable hostel in a cream-and-yellow villa is on a busy road, so best ask for a room off the street. The cheapest doubles have communal showers.

All-Linn (Lower Town)

Hotels and guesthouses

L Hotel Schlossle, Pühavaimu 13/15, **T** 699 7700, **F** 699 7777, www.schlossle-hotels.com. *Map 1, F7, p252* Tallinn's first five-star hotel remains plush, elegant and hugely romantic, with a crackling fire in winter and a private terrace for long summer nights. It's done up in antique English style, with wrought-iron lights and old prints on the walls, and has a homely, intimate atmosphere. Free morning sauna.

L The Three Sisters, Pikk 71, **T** 630 6300, www.threesisters hotel.com. *Map 2, B7, p252* Tallinn's newest five-star boutique hotel, in a trio of cream and yellow medieval merchant houses, has a modern, designer feel, with funky bathroom sinks and large glass windows that sit well with the old beams and vaulted ceilings. The soft cream furnishings are of superb quality, with bathrobes and linen to die for.

A Barons, Suur-Karja 7, **T** 699 9700, **F** 699 9710, www.baronshotel.ee. *Map 2, I6, p253* South of Raekoja plats, this Jugendstil-ish building (1912) used to be a bank, so there's no need to worry about your valuables: they can be stored in the main safe. There's a nostalgic feel, but the rooms are on the small side, and a tad overpriced, although many have Old Town views and underfloor heating in the bathrooms. Suites have their own sauna.

A Domina City, Vana-Posti 11/13, **T** 681 3900, **F** 681 3901, www.dominahotels.com. *Map 2, J6, p253* The former headquarters of the Soviet navy (spot the hammer and sickle on the façade) has been transformed into a sparkling hymn to capitalism, with a glittering lobby and flamboyant marble staircase. The corridors are wide but the rooms, all in beige and brown, are not the largest. Stylish lobby bar, patio garden, sauna and babysitting service.

A Hotel St Petersbourg, Rataskaevu 7, **T** 628 6500, **F** 628 6565, www.schlossle-hotels.com. *Map 2, H4, p253* The Schlossle's sister hotel has a more corporate feel, but the location, opposite the Cat's Well, is superb. Opened in 1850, it was the destination of choice for members of the Moscow nomenklatura during the Soviet era. The top-floor sauna has great Old Town views.

A Imperial, Nunne 14, **T** 627 4800, **F** 627 4801, www.imperial.ee. *Map 2, F4, p253* Northwest of Raekoja plats, this 19th-century building has a section of the Old Town wall running through it: you walk through a gap in it to reach the junior suite. The decor is tasteful, with old maps on the walls and unfussy furnishings.

B Guesthouse Gloria, Müürivahe 2, **T** 644 6950, www.gloria.ee. *Map 2, K5, p253* Above the splendid Gloria restaurant are a handful of cosy rooms, as well as two suites. All are decorated in 1920s and 1930s fashion. There's a hint of kitsch in some of the decor, but the idea of tumbling into bed after a wickedly indulgent meal has distinct appeal. Prices drop dramatically in winter.

B Kalev Spa, Aia 18, **T** 649 3300, **F** 649 3301, www.kalevspa.ee. *Map 2, D/E9, p252* The city's swish new spa complex (see p204) also houses 100 rooms in a crisp, modern style, with wood floors, plasma screens and a fresh, light feel. Guests get free use of the water park, and all manner of massages, masks and spa treatments are available in package or pay-as-you-go formats.

B Merchant's House Hotel, Dunkri 4/6, **T** 697 7500, **F** 697 7501, www.merchantshousehotel.com. *Map 2, H4/5, p253* This charming boutique hotel, near Raekoja plats, combines contemporary chic with a medieval setting. The wooden-floored rooms, which vary substantially in size, are arranged around a pretty inner courtyard. The public areas have 14th-century beamed ceilings and fireplaces.

B Old Town Maestro's, Suur-Karja 10, **T** 626 2000, **F** 631 3333, www.maestrohotel.ee. *Map 2, J5, p253* This former merchant's house, rebuilt in 1928, has high-ceilinged rooms with large mirrors, dark furniture and, in most cases, baths. Children under 12 free.

B Olevi Residents, Olevimägi 4, **T** 627 7650, **F** 627 7651, olevi@olevi.ee. *Map 2, E6, p252* Surprisingly labyrinthine given its narrow Old Town façade, the Olevi Residents has spacious rooms with reproduction antiques that might not be to everybody's taste (think cherubs in gilt frames). Larger suites are ideal for families.

B Taanilinna Hotell, Uus 6, **T** 640 6700, **F** 646 4306, www.taanilinna.ee. *Map 2, G8, p253* Despite the tumbledown surrounds, this quiet hotel is one of Tallinn's most tasteful, with simple white walls and plenty of dark wood. The slightly smaller economy twins are great value (1200 EEK), while the sauna has a chic chill-out room with a CD player. Children under seven free.

B Vana Wiru, Viru 11, **T** 669 1500, **F** 669 1501,
www.vanawiru.ee. *Map 2, H7, p253* Around the corner from
bustling Viru street, this former fashion house announces itself
with a bang. The immodestly glitzy lobby has stained glass and a
white grand piano – Ivana Trump would feel completely at home.
Rooms are not huge, though, and the piped music in the corridors
may set your teeth on edge. Children under seven free.

C Meriton Old Town, Lai 49, **T** 614 1300, **F** 667 7001,
www.meritonhotels.com. *Map 2, B6, p252* Conveniently located
on the edge of the Old Town, in a large 19th-century house. The
public areas are bright and attractive, with sections of the
16th-century city wall incorporated into the design. The
non-smoking rooms, with mock-medieval decor, are on the small
side; most have showers.

D Romeo Family Hotel, Suur-Karja 18, **T/F** 644 4255,
www.hot.ee/hotel. *Map 2, K6, p253* A Russian-run hostelry in a
faded 19th-century block on the southern edge of the Old Town,
with three large, slightly gaudy rooms with bathrooms, and a
pleasant dining room. Old Town apartments are also available.
Children under seven free.

D Villa Hortensia, Vene 6, **T** 504 6113. *Map 2, H6, p253* Part of
the delightfully ramshackle Master's Courtyard complex, near the
ruins of the Dominican Monastery, the 'villa' consists of four small,
simple and charming duplex apartments with wooden furniture
and floors. Above the next-door handicraft gallery, a suite with
kitchen and tiny balcony (1200 EEK) is great for families.

E Old House Guesthouse, Uus 22, **T** 641 1464,
www.oldhouse.ee. *Map 2, D8, p252* Simple rooms on the
northeastern edge of the Lower Town, as well as Old Town
apartment rentals with kitchen and shower for as little as 900 EEK.

Hostels

E Eurohostel, Nunne 2, **T/F** 644 7788, www.eurohostel.ee.
Map 2, F3, p252 Simple but attractive rooms. Guest kitchen.

E Old House Hostel, Uus 26, **T** 641 1281. *Map 2, D8, p252*
Run by the Old House Guesthouse (see above); from 180 EEK.

E Old Town Backpackers, Uus 14, www.hot.ee/oldtown
backpackers. *Map2, F8, p252* A small place but it packs in a sauna
and laundry. Internet access.

F Vana Tom Hostel, Väike-Karja 1, **T** 631 3252, www.hostel.ee.
Map 2, I6, p253 A hugely popular, professionally run hostel with
pristine showers and dormitories. Dormitory beds with breakfast
are 235 EEK. The private room with two separate beds (555 EEK,
extra bed 235 EEK) is ideal for cash-strapped families.

Kesklinn (Centre)

A Radisson SAS, Rävala puiestee 3, **T** 682 3000,
www.radissonsas.com. *Map 3, G7, p255* Near Onion Village, the
Radisson has a rust-coloured chimney that has forever changed
the city's skyline. Inside, however, it's business as usual: tip-top
facilities, thoughtfully designed rooms and attentive service. The
24th-floor terrace café, with superb views over the city and sea, is
open to non-residents in summer from 1600. Free morning sauna,
summer and weekend discounts. No charge for under-17s; play
area and baby-sitting on request.

A Reval Hotel Olümpia, Liivalaia 33, **T** 631 5333, **F** 631 5675,
www.revalhotels.ee. *Map 3, J7, p255* Built for the 1980 Moscow
Olympics (but underused because of the boycotts), this was once
a dowdy hotel for tourists from fellow socialist countries. Not that

you'd guess from the ritzily renovated lobby and top-notch facilities. Ask for a room with a wooden floor. The 26th-floor sauna and fitness centre, with swimming pool, have stunning views, the city's finest. Children under 12 free.

A Scandic Hotel Palace, Vabaduse väljak 3, **T** 640 7300, **F** 640 7299, www.scandic-hotels.com. *Map 3, H3, p255* Built in 1930, this rather grey building on a bustling square was the unofficial residence for western diplomats in the early 1990s, before embassies were established. Most rooms are done in slightly heavy style – too dark, too green – but the seventh-floor doubles are light and airy, with wooden floors. The sauna is free for Hilton Club members. Free parking.

B Scandic Hotel St Barbara, Roosikrantsi 2a, **T** 640 7600, **F** 640 7430, www.scandic-hotels.com. *Map 3, H2, p255* This converted hospital is a handsome limestone building, with high ceilings and public spaces done up in metallic modern style. White walls give the rooms a light, spacious feel. Free parking, but no sauna.

D-E City Guesthouse, Pärnu maantee 10, T/F 628 2236, www.cityguesthouse.ee. *Map 2, K7, p253* If it can't live up to the façade – a handsome Jugendstil structure on the edge of the old town, with a monumental staircase – this clean, simple hostel-cum-hotel does the basics just fine. Dorm beds go for just 250 EEK, doubles with shared facilities for 750 EEK; 1000 EEK gets you a suite, with your own bathroom and plenty of space.

Harbour and around

B Domina Ilmarine, Põhja puiestee 23, **T** 614 0900, **F** 614 0901, www.dominahotels.com. *Map 3, A3, p254* A stylish hotel in a former machine works near the harbour. All rooms are duplex suites with kitchenettes. There's also a glitzy new annex. Sauna with fireplace, babysitting service, secure parking.

C **Metropol**, Mere puiestee 8b, **T** 667 4500, **F** 667 4600, www.metropol.ee. *Map 3, C6, p254* Near the port, this office-block equivalent of Frankenstein's monster is not exactly tasteful (there's a tacky fountain in the lobby and too much green in the colour scheme), but the rooms are large and light; an extra 300 EEK buys a private sauna. Good service. Free morning sauna.

C **Reval Hotel Central**, Narva maantee 7c, **T** 633 9800, **F** 633 9900, www.revalhotels.com. *Map 3, E7 p254* This family-friendly hotel near the port has spacious doubles and family rooms; there's a playroom, and the young 'uns get a present when you check in. The sauna, with a well-designed chill-out room, is one of the best in town; the same goes for the Novell restaurant.

C **Rotermanni**, Mere puiestee 6a, **T** 668 8588, **F** 668 8580, www.rotermanni.ee. *Map 3, C6, p254* Although it's a modern building, on the foundations of a former factory, a quirky interior gives this hotel a warren-like feel. The rooms are plain and big on pine. Bar and sauna. Not to be confused with the adjacent Rotermanni Viking.

D **City Hotel Portus**, Uus-Sadam 23, **T** 680 6600, **F** 680 6601, www.tallinnhotels.ee. *Map 3, A8/9, p254* This port-side hotel describes itself as "young at heart", and so it is. There's an upbeat 1970s look throughout, with a well-equipped playroom in the lobby. There are six family rooms and 12 more with sofa beds, all with showers and WiFi access. Parking is free; you pay extra to use the sauna. The surrounding area is something of a wasteland, but there are cafes nearby, and it's only a 15-minute walk to the Old Town.

Kadriorg

AL-C Villa Stahl, Narva maantee 112, **T** 603 1730 **F** 603 1740, www.villastahl.ee. *Map 1, D8, p251* A stone's throw from the sea, this 1930s villa has been transformed into a unique guesthouse with luxurious suites that cater for a wide range of budgets. The tasteful decor combines Scandic cool with period furniture and there are wood and electric saunas.

D Comfort Hotel Oru, Narva maantee 120b, **T** 603 3302, **F** 601 2600, www.oruhotel.ee. *Map 1, D9, p251* A chain hotel near the Song Festival Grounds, with bland but comfortable rooms. There's a pleasant third-floor terrace and the car park is huge. Free morning sauna.

D Poska Villa, Poska 15, **T** 601 3601, **F** 601 3754, www.hot.ee/poskavilla. *Map 1, H10, p251* On one of the loveliest streets in Kadriorg, this cosy villa has small, bright rooms with light wooden furniture; the great-value apartment (1200 EEK) has a well-equipped kitchen and sleeps up to four.

Pirita

D Brigittine Convent Guesthouse, Merivälja tee 18, **T** 605 5000, **F** 605 5010, www.piritaklooster.ee. *Map 1, B10, p251* The stunning home of the Swedish Brigittine order has impeccable accommodation run by the nuns, most of whom speak English. The single and twin rooms are simple but pristine, with smooth wooden floors. There's a 2100 curfew, but a nun will sit up for latecomers; talk about a test of your Christian charity.

D Pirita Top Spa, Regati puiestee 1, **T** 639 8600, **F** 639 8821, www.topspa.ee. *Map 1, B10, p251* Part of the Moscow Olympics complex, the Top Spa is monumentally monstrous. The small, cabin-like rooms have Brutalist-style concrete balconies; ask for a sea view. So, it's a slice of Soviet history, but what keeps it relevant is the array of modern spa treatments and facilities: 25-m pool, gym, salt chamber, sports hall, even an infra-red sauna.

Kalamaja and Kopli Bay

E Stroomi, Randla 11, Kopli, **T** 630 4200, **F** 630 4500, www.stroomi.ee. *Map 1, C3, p250* The local architecture is decidedly Soviet, the lift's wobbly and there's a kitsch suite with an off-putting painting of a naked woman on the wall, but the standard rooms are adequate and spacious, and it's not far from the beach. Beauty parlour, sauna, parking. Locals advise using taxis at night.

Nõmme and around (Kristiine district)

Accommodation in guesthouses further out is cheaper and often cosier and more characterful than in Tallinn itself, though you may have to fork out for taxis.

Hotels and guesthouses

D Valge Villa, Kännu 26, **T** 651 7450/655 1196, **F** 654 2302, www.white-villa.com. *Map 1, F4, p250* In the heart of the peaceful Kristiine district, 3 km from the centre, this villa has rustic, spacious rooms, a wood-burning sauna and a garden with apple trees. The suite has a kitchen corner, a balcony and, for winter, an open fire. Free parking, free internet access. 10% off online bookings.

E Nepi, Nepi 10, **T** 655 1665, **F** 655 2254, www.nepihotell.ee. *Map 1, F5, p250* A budget hotel with simply furnished rooms, a pretty garden and an apartment (900 EEK), which has a spacious kitchen, a large bedroom and a sofa bed in the lounge. A triple is better value than most hostel dormitories.

F Allee Guesthouse, Tedre 51, **T** 651 3811, **F** 651 3810, www.hot.ee
/allee. *Trolleybuses 2, 3, 4 and 9; buses 17 and 17a. Map 1, F4, p250*
This friendly guesthouse in Kristiine has simple, tasteful rooms with
en suite bathrooms and TVs. Children under four free. Parking.

Hostels

F Academic Hostel, Raja 8/Akadeemia tee 11, **T** 620 2275,
F 620 2276, www.academichostel.com. *Map 1, H2, p250* In
Tallinn's Technical University, this ultra-modern hostel is a real
find. There are cafés and food shops on campus and parking is
available. Book the previous day before 1800 for breakfast.
Shared kitchen and toilet.

Around Tallinn

Viimsi

C Viimsi Tervis Spa Hotel, Randvere tee 11, **T** 606 1000, **F** 606
1003, www.viimsitervis.ee. A spa hotel near the beach, popular
with Scandinavians in search of cheap and anonymous plastic
surgery. The rooms are stylish and calm, with circular windows;
from the upper floors, you can see the Bay of Tallinn. Treatments
on offer include salt chamber (for asthma), paraffin (for aching
joints), light therapy and aroma-massage. Free access to the 25-m
swimming pool and a state-of-the-art fitness centre.

Lahemaa and the north coast

D Kolga Hotel, Kolga, Harjumaa, **T** 607 7477, **F** 607 7270,
www.kolgahotell.ee. Simple but attractive rooms in the former
stables of the Kolga estate. The cheapest have shared toilets and
showers. Children under 12 free.

D Park Hotel, Palmse, **T** 32 23626, **F** 32 34167, www.phpalmse.ee. Fresh, light, pine-clad rooms in the former distillery building of one of the country's most attractive manor estates. Top-floor rooms have lovely lake views; some doubles have baths.

F Rannamänid, Käsmu, Vihula vald, Lääne-Virumaa, Neeme tee 31, **T/F** 32 38329. Attractive guesthouse made from two houses a stone's throw from the beach. There are eight simple rooms, some with shared toilets and showers.

G Musta Kassi Kamping, 723 81, Peterburi maantee, **T** 603 3081, mustakassikorts@hotmail.com. About 30 km east of Tallinn in Kodasoo, this place is easy to find thanks to the red sign at the roadside. It's charming, peaceful and hospitable, with several small chalets (200 EEK per person) and camping spaces (60 EEK) surrounded by forest. Round-the-clock hot water and electricity; on-site café and a rustic sauna house.

Haapsalu

D Fra Mare, Ranna tee 2, **T** 47 24600, **F** 47 24601, www.framare.ee. The usual array of health and beauty treatments, including mud cures, in a large spa hotel near the beach. The endless corridors have a slightly antiseptic feel, but the rooms are spacious and comfortable. Best avoid the restaurant, though.

D Kongo, Kalda 19, **T** 47 24800, **F** 47 24809, www.kongo hotel.ee. Five minutes' walk from the medieval castle, with the most modern and tasteful rooms in town: wooden floors, light-wood furniture and a cream-and-beige colour scheme. Free morning sauna.

D Promenaadi Hotell, Sadama 22, **T** 47 37254, **F** 47 37250
www.promenaadi.ee. Part of this seafront hotel is housed in a
19th-century villa, but it has a modern feel, with garish orange and
blue decor. Free morning sauna, parking, discounts out of season.

Matsalu

E Altmõisa Guesthouse, Tuuru küla, Ridala vald, **T** 47 24680,
F 47 24681, www.altmoisa.ee. On the remote northern coast of
Matsalu Bay – prime birdwatching territory – this eco-friendly
hotel shows the benefits of using locally made furniture, textiles
and natural materials, such as the reed roof. Great value and very
romantic. The restaurant uses organic fruit, vegetables and berries
from the surrounding gardens. Children under seven free.

Vormsi

E Elle-Malle Guest House, **T/F** 47 32072, www.vormsi.ee/
bka/turism/ellemalle.html. This delightful wooden forest house,
with a veranda-style dining room, has rooms in the cottage and a
double in a wobbly-looking windmill (summer only).

Pärnu

Hotels and guesthouses

A Ammende Villa, Mere puiestee 7, **T** 44 73888,
www.ammende.ee. This lavish art nouveau villa is found en route
to the beach. Rooms in the main house are all suites scattered
with appropriately decadent *fin-de-siècle* furniture; those in the
neighbouring gardener's house are cheaper and less cheerful.

B Villa Andropoff, Valgeranna küla, Audru vald, **T** 44 43453, villap@estpak.ee, www.villaandropoff.fi. Yes, that Andropoff: this red-brick edifice near Valgerand beach, 6 km from Pärnu, was built on the orders of the Russian premier, although he died before its completion. It has the slightly gloomy feel of buildings built for the nomenklatura, but the rooms, or rather apartments, are a revelation. For 1900 EEK, you get two spacious double bedrooms, living room, sauna, mini-kitchen, shower, toilet and breakfast. The mini chalets in the grounds (1800 EEK) sleep four and have saunas.

C Scandic Rannahotell, Ranna puiestee 5, **T** 44 32950, **F** 44 32918, www.scandic-hotels.com. Just back from the beach, this ship-shaped hotel is Functionalism at its finest. In the garden stands a tree planted by Lennart Meri, post-Soviet Estonia's first president. Disappointingly, the rooms are business-like and on the small side. It's worth paying extra for a view.

D Inge Villa, Kaarli 20, **T** 44 38510, inge.villa@mail.ee. A pretty wooden villa on a quiet street near the beach. The decor is simple, but the fine pictures on the walls make up for that. Piano, small garden and sauna.

D Pärnu Yachtclub Guesthouse, Lootsi 6, **T** 44 71740, **F** 44 71751, www.jahisadam.ee. Simple, modern rooms, some with views of the marina below. Hospitable atmosphere and a decent restaurant with outside terrace.

Hostels

F Pärnu Hostel Staadioni, Ranna puiestee 2, **T** 44 25799. If you are really cash-strapped and plan to spend most of your time on the beach, this hostel has a good location near the sports stadium.

Kihnu

E Tolli Tourist Farm, T 44 69908, www.kihnutalu.ee. No-frills accommodation in log cabins and a rustic farmhouse. There is a rambling garden, and your hosts can arrange excursions and a private boat to bring you to and from the mainland.

Tartu

Sleeping

Hotels and guesthouses

B Draakon, Raekoja plats 2, T 7 442045, www.draakon.ee. Opposite the town hall, Tartu's smartest hotel is used by celebrities, ambassadors and politicians. Some rooms overlook the students' fountain, others overlook Dome Hill. There is a sauna in the basement.

D Uppsala Maja, Jaani 7, T 7 361535, F 7 361536, www.uppsalamaja.ee. In an 18th-century building, this is by a long shot the most charming place to stay in Tartu. The five non-smoking rooms are spacious: one is ensuite, the others share two toilets, bathrooms and lounge areas. Book two rooms and it's like having your own apartment.

Hostels

D Tartu, Soola 3a, T 7 314300, www.tartuhotell.ee. Tartu's most central hostel, 10 minutes from the town hall and a short hop from the Vanemuine Theatre.

Eating and drinking

Tallinn is packed with eateries serving everything from hearty German-influenced Estonian dishes to fine French cuisine with a local twist. The restaurant scene has developed pretty much from scratch in the past 15 years and establishments come and go at breakneck speed, with many would-be superchefs discovering that they have bitten off more than they can chew. Dining in Tallinn is usually cheap and, at its best, it offers unbelievable value for money, although only a handful of restaurants would truly stand out in New York or London. There's an emphasis on stylish, often spectacular, interior design and presentation, with most new establishments creating a fantastic first impression, although some could do with canning the background music. Service is usually efficient, if stiff, and portions are on the generous side – one course is often enough. Many restaurants are still relatively expensive for locals, so you may find yourself dining only with foreigners or in a spookily empty room.

Eating codes

Price

▐▐▐	300 EEK and over
▐▐	150-300 EEK
▐	150 EEK and under

Prices given here are per head for two courses, excluding drinks. Tips are optional, but a tip of 10% is usually expected.

Upmarket dining is sometimes intimidatingly formal, with service so attentive it can be claustrophobic. For something a little earthier, try such quintessentially Estonian dishes as pork with sauerkraut and roast potatoes, Baltic herring, broth with dumplings and meatballs, beetroot salad, jellied veal, cottage cheese or blood pudding. Eating hours are flexible, with many locals lunching as late as 1500. Dinner is usually served until 2200.

Toompea

Restaurants

▐▐▐ **Cathedral**, Lossi plats 2/Toomkooli 1, **T** 644 3548, www.cathedral.ee. *Mon-Sat 1200-1100, Sun 1200-1800. Map 2, J1, p253* A formal, elegant restaurant frequented by businessmen and MPs. The menu features Russian and French cuisine and is long on alcohol-flavoured dishes: mussels in wine, frogs' legs with cognac, grilled trout with white wine , veal with calvados.

▐▐ **Le Paris**, Toompuiestee 27, **T** 667 7105, www.meriton.ee. *0630-2200. Map 1, D5, p250* Top-notch international cuisine is on the menu at the Meriton Grand Hotel's ground-floor restaurant. The weekday lunch buffet – cold meats, salads and fish – is amazingly good value, at 95 EEK for the hot or cold buffet and 150 EEK for both.

143

Made in Estonia

Spiced, salted sprats have long been part of the Estonian diet. So ubiquitous are the sprat tins marked with the silhouette of the Old Town that one of the city's nicknames is Spratsville. They are an acquired taste, but one worth persevering with. Fresh local fish, sadly, is in short supply for a port; much of the catch winds up on the Norwegian fish market.

Pork, beef and dairy products are particularly good here, as are native wild berries and mushrooms (the chanterelles are exquisite). Lamb, however, often means mutton, so do ask what you're getting. If you want your meat rare, say "very rare!". Local sausages and ham are generally heavily smoked. Most dairy produce is excellent, although Estonian cheeses are too mild for some tastes. Bread is generally good, especially the sour, long-lasting rye bread, a feature of every Estonian table worth its salt. Traditionally, lining the bottom of the oven with cabbage leaves produces the best results. The importance of bread is underlined by the traditional greeting when encountering people at table: "May your bread last!"

Kama, or soured milk, is another classic Estonian comestible. Try *kali*, a dark-brown sweetish non-alcoholic drink made of bread, malt, rye or oats, flour and yeast.

Estonians are great coffee-drinkers (some say it's to do with those long, dark winter nights, which you can only get through with an extra kick) and coffee is usually served strong. Herbal and organic teas are also popular.

Pika Jala Restoran, Pikk jalg 16, **T** 644 1344, www.pikajala.ee. *Mon-Sat 1000-2300, Sun 1000-2200. Map 2, I3, p253* There's a French emphasis to the food at this trendy restaurant with a bright exposed-brick interior. Try blinis with red caviar and smoked trout, prawns with pike mousse and savoy cabbage or fillet steak.

¶ **Toomkooli Tõllad**, Toomkooli 13, **T** 644 6613, www.toom kooli.ee. *1200-2400. Map 2, I1, p253* Rustic atmosphere, views across the city to the sea, salads, herring, pork with apple and ginger.

Cafés

Bogapott, Pikk jalg 9, **T** 631 3181. *Summer 1000-1900, winter 1000-1800. Map 2, I3, p253* A café-cum-art gallery by the city wall. Admire the ceramics as you snack on generous sandwiches or tasty cakes.

Mademoiselle, in the Meriton Grand Hotel Tallinn, Toompuiestee 27, **T** 667 7150, www.grandhotel.ee. *0700-2200. Map 1, D5, p250* A good spot for salads, soups and freshly made quiches, cakes and pastries.

Neitsitorn, Lühike jalg 9a, **T** 644 0514. *1000-2000, cash only. Map 2, J3, p253* An essential Tallinn experience: have a coffee or a beer out on the ramparts of the city walls, with peerless views across the Old Town.

All-Linn

Restaurants

¶¶¶ **Balthasar**, Raekoja plats 11, **T** 627 6400, www.restaurant.ee. *Daily 1200-2400. Map 2, G6, p253* 'Garlic restaurant' above Raeapteek, with beamed ceilings and fine views over the townhall square. Dishes are rated on a bulb scale: at the high end, an appetizer with whole cloves doused in chilli, pesto, curry and

★ Restaurants with a view

balsamic vinegar is so overpowering, it makes your eyeballs flicker. To drink, what else but garlic vodka?

Le Bonaparte, Pikk 45, **T** 646 4444, www.bonaparte.ee. *Mon-Sat 1200-1500, 1900-2400. Map 2, E6, p252* This thoroughly French restaurant is one of Tallinn's best eateries; President Chirac ate here during an official visit in 2001. Dine on duck fillet with raspberry syrup and asparagus, pike-perch with champagne and almonds, or chanterelles and garlic soup, in a delightful 17th-century interior.

Bocca, Olevimägi 9, **T** 641 2610, www.bocca.ee. *1200-2400. Map 2, D7, p252* Ultra-stylish, if slightly pricey Italian, frequented by foreign dignitaries and fashionable locals. Faultless presentation in a vaulted setting with glorious lights. Favourite dishes include tuna carpaccio with avocado, smoked deer with rocket and Parmesan, or tarragon- flavoured vineyard snails.

Egoist, Vene 33, **T** 646 4052, www.egoist.ee. *1200-2400 Map 2, D7, p252* Like its celebrated sister restaurant, Gloria, Egoist harks back to the halcyon days of the First Republic. With romantic nooks and a plush, luxurious feel, it has a winter feel and is a favourite birthday venue for locals who can afford it. The cooking is rich and traditional: lobster carpaccio, game and rack of lamb.

Eating and drinking

¶¶¶ **Gloria**, Müürivahe 2, **T** 644 6950, www.gloria.ee. *1200-2330. Map 2, K5, p253* More pre-war nostalgia, this time entirely genuine. The resolutely retro interior is plush with crimson furnishings, the food is a mix of French and Russian classics, and there are nods to local tradition and Italian cuisine: borscht, duck, sole and lamb. The best wine cellar in the Baltics to boot.

¶¶¶ **Karl Friedrich**, Raekoja plats 5, **T** 627 2413, www.restaurant.ee. *1000-2400. Map 2, H5, p253* Famed for its fish dishes, this former pre-war café is named after the founder of the Saku brewery. Try plaice with shrimps and sparkling wine, marinated eel or mussels in white wine.

¶¶¶ **Nevskij**, Rataskaevu 7, **T** 628 6560, www.schlossle-hotels.com. *1200-1500, 1800-2300. Map 2, H4, p253* In the upmarket St Petersbourg Hotel, this is one of the classiest Russian restaurants in town. The cooking and presentation are superb, the surroundings are cosy, plush and decidedly pre-revolutionary, and the service is almost too attentive. Try delicate *pelmeni* (dumplings) with garlic butter and meltingly tender beef stroganoff. Complimentary shots of vodka are served throughout, so go easy on the wine.

¶¶¶ **Pegasus**, Harju 1, **T** 631 4040, www.restoranpegasus.ee. *Mon-Thu 0800-0100, Fri 0800-0200, Sat 1000-0200. Map 2, J5, p253* For most locals, this is the place to see and be seen. Try carpaccio of Muhu ostrich with mango, scallops with asparagus, lamb curry, sea bass with truffle sausage or beef with morel mushrooms. Great views from the upstairs section.

¶¶¶ **Stenhus**, Pühavaimu 13/15, **T** 699 7780, www.schlossle-hotels.com. *0700-1100, 1200-1500, 1900-2230. Map 2, F6, p253* Refined but not too stuffy, the Hotel Schlössle's restaurant serves five-star food in an impossibly romantic vaulted cellar. Try turbot tartare with tomato, dill, rocket salad and truffle juice or baked langoustine and crayfish tails with saffron cream sauce.

¶¶ **Aed**, Rataskaevu 8, **T** 626 9088. *Mon-Sat 1200-2200, Sun 1200-1800. Map 2, H4, p253* The 'Embassy of Pure Food' melds mod-Med and Estonian cooking in a plant-filled, medieval setting, with organic produce taking pride of place. In a city where restaurants celebrate the pleasures of the flesh, this is a veggie haven, offering porridge casserole with lentil and pumpkin, risotto with zucchini and dried fruits and wok-cooked vegetable dishes, alongside Baltic herring soup and a smattering of meat dishes.

¶¶ **Controvento**, Vene 12, **T** 644 0470. *1200-2300. Map 2, G8, p253* Beloved of Italian expats and tourists, Controvento is home to the best *vitello tonnato* in the Baltics. The restaurant has cool white walls trimmed with red and green, a calm space in which to concentrate on the food. Service can be arrogant: expect a public dressing-down if you don't book ahead.

¶¶ **KN**, Dunkri 4/6, **T** 697 7510, www.merchantshousehotel.com. *1100-2300. Map 2, H4/5, p253* An upmarket restaurant, attached to the Merchant's House Hotel, where the British chef makes the most of market-fresh produce, serving Franco-Italian dishes such as duck confit, wild mushroom risotto, tuna steak *niçoise* and steak Rossini with foie gras and truffle mash. There's a delightful terrace in the whitewashed courtyard, concealed from the Old Town crowds.

¶¶ **Kuldse Notsu Kõrts**, Dunkri 8, **T** 628 6567, www.schlossle-hotels.com. *1200-2400. Map 2, H4, p253* Pleasant street-side terrace, porcine window boxes and a refined rustic-style interior with apposite Estonian sayings daubed on the walls. The food is traditional and solid – bacon-laced bread, giant knuckles of pork with mustard, wild boar with juniper berry sauce, pig's ears, fried liver, meat jelly – but prices are rather high.

★ Restaurants with terraces

Best

- Pika Jala p144
- Balthasar, p145
- KN p148
- Vertigo p154

♗♗ Maikrahv, Raekoja plats 8, **T** 631 4227, www.maikrahv.ee. *1200-2300. Map 2, H5, p253* Upmarket cellar restaurant serving inventive dishes such as piglet with sage, polenta and cider sauce, as well as old Estonian favourites like blood sausage with sauerkraut, on silver platters, no less. Occasional live classical music.

♗♗ Meister Michel, Rataskaevu 22, **T** 641 3414, www.meister michel.ee. *Map 2, H4, p253 1200-2300.* Another atmospheric vaulted cellar, but one that's decidedly modern in look, with subtle green lighting, apple-green glasses and fake apples decorating the walls. The apple theme runs through the menu, too: roast duck with sautéed savoy cabbage and apple-pear sauce, pork fillet with apple ketchup or pike-perch with a cider-sabayon sauce. For dessert, try the heavenly apple ice cream. Children's menu available.

♗♗ Mõõkkala, Kuninga 4, **T** 641 8288. *1200-2400. Map 3, E/F3, p254* This popular and atmospheric seafood cellar restaurant (booking essential for dinner) offers earthy dishes like herrings in batter or refined ones such as crayfish with an oriental touch.

♗♗ Must Lammas, Sauna 2, **T** 644 2031, www.mustlammas.ee. *Mon-Sat 1200-2300, Sun 1200-1800. Map 2, I7, p253* Formal but friendly and clutter-free, the Black Sheep transports you to Georgia via the food rather than the decor. Carnivores will savour the shasliks, spicy beef balls and piquant lamb soup, but veggies will be relieved to find roasted Georgian cheese with cowberry, marinated eggplant and cabbage roll with mushrooms among the options. Adventurous wine buffs should try a sweet Georgian red.

♯♯ Olde Hansa, Vanaturu kael 1, **T** 627 9020, www.oldehansa.com. *1100-2400. Map 2, J6, p253* The off-Raekoja location, medieval theme and crowded summer terrace may scream tourist trap, but this place is as popular with Tallinners as foreigners. The menu reflects the cosmopolitan nature of Hanseatic Tallinn – Andalusian salmon, slow-baked Wittenberg pork in beer, dried elk meat with juniper-ripened beef. Portions are huge, and best washed down with a pot of honeyed beer.

♯♯ Sisalik, Pikk 30, **T** 646 6542, www.sisaliku.ee. *Mon-Sat 1200-2300. Map 2, E6, p252* Considering its location in the heart of the Old Town, this cellar restaurant with a tapas bar at the front is surprisingly tourist-free. Provençal and Italian food with a strong local flavour is served in a warm vaulted interior with lemon walls: prawns flambéed in cognac, grilled tuna with cucumber wasabi, pike-perch in cream and excellent steaks. Children's menu.

♯♯ Tanduur, Vene 7, **T/F** 631 3084, www.tanduur.ee. *1200-2400. Map 2, H6, p253* One of the few decent ethnic eateries in Tallinn. It's dimly lit, refreshingly flock-free and, for those used to the bhajis-and-lager culture of British curry houses, off-puttingly formal. The dishes are generous, tasty and properly spiced, if a little pricey. A good takeaway option if you are self-catering.

♯♯ The Three Sisters, Pikk 71/Tolli 2, **T** 630 6300, www.three sistershotel.com. *Map 2, B7, p252* This cellar restaurant offers a fairly formal dining experience with an unfussy frill-free decor. With an emphasis on fresh produce, the menu is creative and changes seasonally. Past delights include a seriously silky pumpkin purée soup and one of the best pork dishes in Tallinn: piglet marinated in cider and served with a red wine and chanterelle sauce.

Troika, Raekoja plats 15, **T** 627 6245, www.troika.ee. *1200-2300. Map 2, H6, p253* Tallinn's most popular Russian restaurant has a terrace on the main square and a stunning vaulted interior that takes you straight back to Tsarist times. Serving staples such as *pelmeni*, beef stroganoff, pancakes and salmon pie, it's less refined than nearby Nevskij, but it's also less stuffy and good value for money. Occasional live Russian folk music.

Vanaema Juures, Rataskaevu 10/12, **T** 626 9080. *Mon-Sat 1200-2200, Sun 1200-1800. Map 2, H4, p253* Grandma's Place is a cellar restaurant with a suitably homely feel. The background pop music jars, but the food is quality Estonian fare: tender meatballs and succulent fillets of pork with some of the best sauerkraut in town.

Sushi Baar Silk, Kullassepa 4, **T** 648 4625. *1200-2400. Map 2, H5, p253* Aimed squarely at Tallinn's smarter set, with minimalist Japanese-style decor and ambient music. The sushi is up to scratch, but the real thrill comes from seeing the self-conscious clientele trying to maintain their cool while wrestling with the chopsticks.

African Kitchen, Uus 34, **T** 644 2555, www.africankitchen.ee. *1200-0100, Fri-Sat till 0200. Map 2, C8, p252* The 'street of the unexpected' springs yet another surprise, in the form of Tallinn's first African restaurant. Even more unexpectedly, it's a cracker, with tribal designs on the walls, low lighting and plenty of room to stretch out and relax. Try fish or beef in coconut or peanut sauce, spicy jollof rice or peri peri chicken wings. On Friday and Saturday nights, the roots, dub and reggae sounds get even the normally reserved Estonians shaking their tushes.

Bakuu, Harju7/9, **T** 699 9680, www.bakuu.ee. *1000-2400, Fri-Sat -0200, Sun 1100-2300. Map 2, J5, p253* Azerbaijani cuisine (and music) in a pretty medieval setting. It's especially good for *shasklik* (kebabs), but be warned: the portions are humungous.

¶ **Beer House**, Dunkri 5, **T** 627 6520, www.beerhouse.ee. *Sun-Thu 1000-2400, Fri and Sat 1000-0200; first floor daily 1100-2300, Fri and Sat 1100-0400, live music Fri and Sat. Map 2, H5, p253* Tallinn's only microbrewery is a vast, country-style hall. It's a friendly, down-to-earth place, the beers are good and the food is unfussy and filling: hunter's sausages, chicken kiev and prodigiously large pizzas. Shoestring travellers will love the lunchtime happy hour (1200-1400), when food and beer are half price: a pizza and a pint will set you back just 55 EEK.

¶ **Da Vinci**, Aia 7, **T** 641 6177, www.davincifood.ee. *Map 2, H9, p253* This straightforward restaurant with a vaguely modern Mediterranean-style interior serves good, reasonably priced pizzas and bruschetta, as well as superb home-made pasta (try the tortellini in a rich, nutty sauce). There's a small roadside terrace.

Cafés

Angel, Sauna 1, **T** 641 6880. *Mon-Wed 1200-0200, Thu-Sat till late, Sun 1400-0100. Map 2, I7, p253* Next to the gay club of the same name, this smart but relaxed upstairs café-bar is ideal for an afternoon coffee or a couple of pre-clubbing drinks. There are discreet nooks for longer lingering, and everyone is welcome (the toilets are labelled "homo" and "hetero"). Good range of dance tunes, inexpensive snacks and super smoothies.

Anneli Viik, Pikk 30, **T** 644 4530, www.anneliviik.ee. *1100-2300, Sun -1900. Map 2, E6, p252* Exquisite handmade chocolates are the speciality at this cosy Old Town café/shop. A handful of tables offer views of Pikk street or of the chocolatiers at work in the open kitchen. As a winter warmer, the hot chocolate is out of this world.

Café Aroma, Pikk 12, **T** 648 7210, www.baltisepik.ee. *0730-2100. Map 2, G5, p253* The chief draw here is the extensive choice of exotic coffees: where else in the world will you have the chance to try coffee laced with the treacly Vana Tallinn liqueur?

Café Bonaparte, Pikk 45, **T** 646 4444, www.bonaparte.ee. *Mon-Sat 0800-2200, Sun 1000-1800 Map 2, E6, p252* An upmarket, white-walled café in a gorgeous medieval building that echoes the quality of the attached restaurant, Le Bonaparte (p146). Excellent quiches and the best patisserie in town. Great for breakfast.

Chocolaterie, Vene 6 (Meistrite hoov), **T** 641 8061. *Mon-Fri 1100-2300, Sat and Sun 1000-2400, cash only. Map 2, H6, p253* In a charmingly tumbledown old courtyard, this is a great spot for tea, hot chocolate, coffee or liqueur, not to mention handmade chocolates. The 19th-century decor is romantically nostalgic.

Illusioon, Müürivahe 50/Uus 3, **T** 641 9833, www.tujutoit.ee. *1000-2300. Map 2, G8, p253* The florid Kinomaja (Cinema House) is the place to go if you want to meet film students. Casual, cheap and mildly bohemian, it serves snacks like omelettes and seljanka soup.

Kehrwieder, Saiakang 1. *Sun-Thu 0900-2300, Fri and Sat 0900-0100. Cash only. Map 2, G5, p253* Cavernous cellar café just off Raekoja, with decadent divans and thick-topped wooden tables for those who prefer to stay vertical. Excellent coffees, teas and organic brews.

Robert's Café, Viru 13/15, **T** 631 4750. *1000-2000. Map 2, H7, p253* On the top floor of the *De la Gardie* shopping complex, this café has a modern, funky feel, with good views of the bustling Old Town below. Seriously good coffee and simple sandwiches.

Tristan ja Isolde, Raekoja plats 1, **T** 644 0818. *Sun-Thu 0800-2300, Fri and Sat 0800-0100. Cash only. Map 2, H5, p253* Charming, intimate café-cum-bar with tables under the town hall arcade. Excellent coffee and some of the best background music in town.

Kesklinn (Centre)

Restaurants

♦♦♦ Vertigo, Rävala puistee 4, **T** 53 494222, www.vertigo.ee.
0900-2400. Map 3, H5, p255 Imre Kose is Estonia's leading chef, and
this is his long-awaited new restaurant. As the name suggests, it's
several floors up in a brand-new building, with panoramic views of
the city from the rooftop terrace. The interior includes wooden
floors, black carpets and the odd gold wall. The menu offers local
produce jazzed up with mod-Med flair: tartare of wild mushrooms
and smoked elk, pan-fried ostrich liver with port and caper sauce,
juniper-smoked carré of lamb with oven-roasted beetroot, pear soup
with gorgonzola and pecan ice cream. Best to book in advance.

♦♦ Moskva, Vabaduse Väljak 10, **T** 640 4694, www.moskva.ee.
Map 2, L5, p253 Though Moskva is better known for its club and
café, the restaurant at this fashionably multi-faceted establishment
is a triumph of substance over style. The black walls with red neon
trim are trendy, but not annoyingly so, the atmosphere is relaxed
and the imaginative dishes are served on stylized white dishes.
Sink into a comfy armchair and tuck into local beef with
gorgonzola or smoked trout salad with cottage cheese.

♦ Baieri Kelder, Roosikrantsi 2a, **T** 640 7425, www.scandic-
hotels.com. *1200-2300. Map 3, H2, p255* This atmospheric,
Bavarian-style red-brick cellar serves generous portions of
good-quality sausages, dumplings and sauerkraut.

♦ Eesti Maja, Lauteri 1, **T** 645 5252, www.eestimaja.ee,
1100-2300, buffet lunches Mon-Fri 1100-1500. Map 3, H6, p255
A long-standing Estonian favourite, this eatery near the Foreign
Ministry is the place to go for authentic peasant fare: cabbage or

bean soup, spiced sprats, pearl barley, marinated eel and sinful deep-fried garlic bread. Very reasonable lunch buffet during the week (75 EEK).

Haldjas, Maakri 23a, **T** 661 3029. *Map 3, H7, p255* A no-frills, self-service joint in the heart of Tallinn's financial district, with prices to suit Estonians, not tourists. Soups, stroganoff, stuffed pork cutlets and a salad buffet pull in office workers from the surrounding skyscrapers, so you get a slice of local life with your meal.

Cafés

Bestseller, 3rd floor, Viru Centre, **T** 610 1397. *Daily 0900-2100. Map 3, E6, p254* Run by Imre Kosea, of Vertigo (see p154), this is a super café in one corner of the city's best bookshop. The decor is bright, white and modern, with a cheery tartan banquette. The atmosphere is laid-back, and the light salads, sandwiches and pasta dishes make inventive use of top-quality ingredients and home-made dressings. Kose sometimes pops in to serve at the bar: in this reticent city, his exuberant, flamboyant presence stands out a mile.

Café VS, Pärnu maantee 28, **T** 627 2627, www.cafevs.ee. *Mon-Thu 1000-0100, Fri 1000-0300, Sat 1200-0300, Sun 1300-0100. Map 3, I3, p255* It's past the first flush of fashionability, but this lively café-cum-bar-cum-eatery serves great Indian food and Tallinn's finest selection of teas. With DJs on Thursdays, Fridays and Saturdays, it's as close as you can get to a clubby atmosphere in daylight.

Kuku Kohvik, Vabaduse väljak 8, **T** 644 5926. *Mon-Fri 0800-2200, Sat and Sun 0900-2100. Map 3, G3, p255* This inexpensive café prides itself on being artsy, although locals of a certain age say it's lost the edge it had during the Soviet era.

Harbour and around

Restaurants

Map 2, D6, p254 — *part of entries below*

¶¶¶ **Ö**, Mere puiestee 6e, **T** 661 6150, www.restoran-o.ee. *1200-2400. Map 2, D6, p254* With spare, stylish black-and-white decor, this airy eatery in a former industrial building near the port is the fashionistas' favourite. Impeccably presented international and Japanese cuisine: good sushi and soups, plus red mullet with olives, pan-fried foie gras with lemon grass and veal with calvados.

¶¶¶ **Admiral**, Lootsi 15, **T** 662 3777, www.aurulaev-admiral.ee. *1200-2300. Map 3, B8, p254* A romantic setting on a steamship. Good house vodka and seafood with a Balkan and Russian twist. Children's menu.

¶¶¶ **Novell**, Narva maantee 7, **T** 633 9891, www.revalhotels.com. *1200-2300. Map 3, E8, p254* The wittily retro decor and seriously creative cuisine at this hotel restaurant attract a well-heeled crowd. Top-notch, reasonably priced dishes include smoked quail with plum salsa, lamb with caponata and raisin pilaf, and pork fillet roll with pepperoni and a salami and pesto stuffing. The desserts are equally imaginative: try carrot and pistachio ice cream.

¶ **Reval Express Café**, Sadama 1, **T** 667 8700, www.reval hotels.com. *1200-2100 Map 3, A6, p254* The Reval Express Hotel's ground-floor eatery is a haven for budget travellers: the all-you-can-eat soup buffet, at 45 EEK, features five soups a day, such as minestrone, pea and ham and borscht.

¶ **Šeš-Beš**, Gonsiori 9. *Mon-Thu 1000-0100, Fri and Sat 1000-0200, Sun 1100-2300. Map 3, F8, p254* Decent, inexpensive kebabs cooked over an open fire.

Cafés

Café Spirit, Mere puiestee 6e, **T** 661 6151, www.kohvikspirit.ee. *Mon-Thu 1200-2300, Fri and Sat 1200-0100, Sun 1300-2200. Map 3, C5, p254* It's not easy to find this oh-so-fashionable café in an old warehouse near the port, presumably because they don't want too many tourists. (Just so you know, it's at the back of the building, on the left.) It's worth seeking out, though: a calm, sleek place in neutral colours, serving sushi and some splendid salads.

Kompass, Reval Central Hotel, Narva Maantee 7c, **T** 633 9811. *Mon-Fri 0900-2000, Sat 1000-2000, Sun 1000-1800. Map 3, E8, p254* As you'd expect from a café on the same site as the excellent Novell restaurant (see p156), this funky eatery serves way-above-average snacks and salads in a jovial atmosphere.

Narva Kohvik, Narva maantee 10, **T** 660 1786. *Mon-Fri 0900-2000, Sat 1000-2000, Sun 1000-1800. Map 3, E8, p254* A decidedly old-fashioned, no-frills hang-out that still has the feel of the Soviet days, but serves a mean *pirozhki* (Russian pie) and is well known for its huge, cream-filled pretzels.

Kadriorg

Restaurants

♈♈♈ **Lydia**, Koidula 13a, **T** 626 8990, www.lydia.ee. *Mon-Sat 1200-2300, Sun 1200-1900. Map 1, E8, p251* Don't be put off by the drab exterior – inside is an evocative 1930s interior with a conservatory and tasteful pictures on the walls. The cooking is classic but inventive: salmon fillet with chilli and lime, ostrich fillet with blackcurrant port, beef with whisky. Children's menu.

♔♔ Restoran Kadriorg, Weizenbergi 18, **T** 601 3636, www.restorankadriorg.ee. *Map 1, D7, p251* Chic Scandinavian-style interior with an open grill, a fireplace and trendy background music. It serves impressive international cuisine, with good fish and a divine duck breast with honey glaze; there's pizza and pasta on offer in a more informal section, too.

Cafés

Kadriorg Palace Café, Weizenbergi 37, **T** 606 6400. *Tue-Sun 1000-1700. Map 1, D8, p251* Coffee and cakes in old-fashioned, frilly surroundings. One of the few places to pause in Kadriorg.

Pirita

Restaurants

♔♔♔ Charital, Kloostri tee 6, **T** 623 7379. *1200-2400. Map 1, B10, p251* Pirita's top restaurant aspires to ancien régime elegance but, feels a bit nouveau riche. The food, with an emphasis on fish and lobster, is impeccably presented. Try artichoke salad with brie, salmon carpaccio with caviar, plum-stuffed rabbit or trout with mushroom sauce. Children's menu.

Cafés

Bellevue, above Charital, Kloostri tee 6. *Map 1, B10, p251* The café above the Charital restaurant has equally attractive riverside views and serves cheap snacks, salads and soups.

Kalevi Jahtklubi, Pirita tee 17, **T** 623 9158. *1100-2200. Map 1, B10, p251* The Kalev Yacht Club's genial bar is a great place to stoke up after a stroll on sand or snow, with suitably nautical decor and a cosy fire at its centre. The food is simple but satisfying: hearty *seljanka* soup, pickled herring and tender *pelmeni* (mini meat pasties).

Kalamaja and Kopli Bay

Cafés

Kolu Kõrts, Rocca al Mare. *Map 1, E1, p250* Plain, peasanty Estonian fare in a convincing tavern-style setting near the entrance to the open-air museum.

Nõmme

℣ **Pirosmani**, Üliõpilaste tee 1, **T** 639 3246, www.restaurant-pirosmani.com. *1000-0100. Map 1, H2, p250* Named after a Georgian painter, this rustic, candle-lit restaurant offers classic Caucasian cooking, with an emphasis on grills.

West of Tallinn: Viimsi

℣ **Jussi Õlletuba**, Liilia 2, Viimsi, **T** 623 8696, www.jussigrupp.ee. *Mon-Thu 1100-2400, Fri and Sat 1100-0100, Sun 1100-2200.* Typical local fare – pork chop with baked cheese, *pelmeni*, fried perch, rye bread fried in garlic – is served in the garden of this friendly inn near the sea. The portions are decidedly large. Occasional live music.

℣ **Paat**, Rohuneeme tee 53, Viimsi, **T/F** 609 0840. *Sun-Thu 1000-2400, Fri and Sat 1000-0200.* This seafront restaurant-cum-bar resembling an overturned boat has views of the Bay of Tallinn. Solid Estonian pub grub: pork and fish with loads of potatoes.

Lahemaa

⚑ **Altja Kõrts**, Altja, **T** 32 58681. *Summer daily, winter on weekends*. This atmospheric old tavern, where travellers, seafarers, trades and salesmen used to gather, serves traditional coastal food.

⚑ **Café Isabella**, Palmse Estate. This dreamy lakeside café, in a former bath house with an ornate domed ceiling, serves simple snacks, salads and drinks.

⚑ **Kolga Hotel**, Kolga Estate, **T** 60 77252, www.kolgahotell.ee. *Daily 1200-2300.* This is one of the poshest places to dine in Lahemaa, though it's still relatively cheap. The European menu offers steamed white fish with celery, roast duckling, mushroom soup and pheasant. Children's menu.

⚑ **Palmse Distillery**, Palmse Estate, **T/F** 32 34167. Salads, omelettes, herring and beef stroganoff are served in a cavernous, candle-lit basement with a roaring fire in winter. Children's menu.

Pärnu

Restaurants

⚑⚑⚑ **Ammende Villa**, Mere puiestee 7, **T** 44 73888, www.ammende.ee. *Sun-Thu 1200-2400, Fri and Sat 1200-0100.* This wonderfully restored Art Nouveau hotel is also home to one of Estonia's most romantic restaurants, whether you eat in the opulent dining rooms or out on the garden terrace. The French-meets-oriental cuisine is inspired.

⚑⚑ **Scandic Rannahotell**, Ranna puiestee 5, **T** 44 32945. *1200-2400.* More minimalist than *Ammende Villa*, but no less stylish, this light, cleanly designed restaurant just behind the beach offers extremely accomplished food at surprisingly reasonable prices. Eat outside rather than in if possible, as the main dining area is a little stuffy.

Seegi Maja, Hospidali 1, **T** 44 30550. *1100-2400*. Inspired by Pärnu's Hanseatic heyday, with a candle-lit interior, wine served in goblets and waiters in medieval dress. The house speciality, only for unreconstructed carnivores, is baked bear in honey.

Kuursaal, Mere puiestee 22, **T** 44 20367, www.parnu kuursaal.ee. *1200-0100*. A wooden tavern with a cheerfully chaotic atmosphere. Expect stomach-lining, rib-sticking Estonian fare: herring and mash, pork with wild mushrooms, beer and pasta.

Steffani Pizzarestoran, Nikolai 24, **T** 44 31170. *1100-2400*. An easy-going place with a terrace overlooking St Elisabeth's. The service is unusually relaxed, children are welcomed, and the pizzas are more than decent.

Cafés

Café Grand, Kuninga 25, **T** 44 43412, www.hot.ee/victoria. A pleasant place to pass an hour or so, whether you're admiring the 1920s decor or watching the world through the large windows.

Jazz Café, Ringi 11, **T** 44 27546, www.abijoon.ee. *Mon-Sat 0900-2400, Sun 0900-2200*. Simple, healthy snacks: trout salad with broccoli, wok-fried vegetables. Live music on Friday evenings.

Yacht Club, Lootsi 6, **T** 44 71940, www.jahisadam.ee. *1000-2400*. A good snack spot: inexpensive but excellent fish dishes are on offer at the local yacht club. You can dine while watching the boats on Pärnu River's small marina.

Haapsalu

¶-¶¶ Kuursaal, Promenaadi 1, **T** 47 35505, www.kuursaal.ee. *May-Sep daily 1000-0200.* The lovely wooden Kuursaal has a menu crammed with bizarrely named dishes such as 'Dr Hunnius' Manoeuvres' (vodka shot, pickles and honey, named after the doctor who researched the curative properties of mud). The food, thankfully, is far from gimmicky.

Tartu

¶ Entri, Rüütli 9, **T** 740 9222, www.entri.ee. Vaulted cellar restaurant in the London Hotel, serving heart soups and casseroles, aswell as local delicacies, such as roasted elk.

¶ Kohvik Werner, Ülikooli 11, **T** 744 1274. *Mon-Sat 1200-2200, Sun 1200-2000.* Opposite the university, this atmospheric café has been in business since 1895. On the menu you'll find staple Estonian dishes like herring with sour cream and boiled potatoes.

¶ Püssirohukelder, Lossi 28, **T** 730 3555, www.pyss.ee. *Mon-Thu 1200-0200, Fri and Sat 1200-0300, Sun 1200-2400.* Vast tavern in an 18th-century brick-walled gunpowder cellar, with large, chunky tables, baskets, barrels, live Estonian music and an outside courtyard terrace. Main courses are huge and hearty, and come with mountains of potatoes. Try the house red beer.

¶ Teatrikohvik, Vanemuise 6, **T** 744 0140, *Sun-Thu 1000-2300, Fri and Sat 1000-0300.* Has a terrace with panoramic views of the city.

¶ Wilde, Vallikraavi 4, **T** 730 9764, www.wilde.ee. *Mon-Sat 1000-2100, Sun 1000-1800.* A converted 19th-century printworks. Besides classic pub fare, there's steak flambéed in Irish whiskey and Tipperary mincemeat pie. Excellent coffees, too.

Eating and drinking

Pre-war Tallinn, they say, never slept, not even in winter. After the blip of the Soviet era, that is pretty much the case again, and the city is a paradise for 24-hour party people. By Western standards, admission and drinks are a bargain, and Tallinn is compact and easily navigable, no matter what state you're in. The introverted Estonians seem to lose their reserve when it comes to a night out, although most venues attract an up-for-it, unpretentious crowd. Most of the megaclubs stick to tried-and-trusted techno hits, but you'll find more sophisticated sounds in the hippest places, and more idiosyncratic music policies in the Old Town's late-night cellar bars. Tallinn also has a vibrant live music scene. Mutant Disco, www.mutantdisco.com, is a good party organizer, staging house, techno, hip-hop, drum'n'bass and jazz nights, mainly at Club Privé. You can find flyers in Café Moskva, Pegasus, Stereo and other trendy cafés, or visit www.stereo88.com/events for details of what's on. Also check out *Von Krahl*, www.vonkrahl.ee, for some of the best parties in town and www.sewercide.ee for alt-rock affairs.

All-Linn

Bars

Avenüü, Suur-Karja 10, **T/F** 644 1019, www.clubavenue.ee.
Map 2, J6, p253 Renovated in early 2006, this Parisian-themed bar stays open 24/7 and gets more random as the night wears on. A good spot for post-club munchies.

Beer House, Dunkri 5, **T** 627 6520, www.beerhouse.ee. *Mon and Tue 1000-2400, Wed and Thu 1000-0200, Fri and Sat 1000-0400. Map 2, H5, p253* Tallinn's only microbrewery, with reasonably authentic German brews from 30 EEK (or 15 EEK at lunchtime). Too big to get truly raucous; dancefloor upstairs.

Depeche Mode, Nunne 4, **T** 641 1608, edmfk.cafe.ee/dmbaar. *Mon-Thu 1200-0100, Fri 1200-0400, Sat 1600-0400, Sun 1600-0100. Map 2, F4, p252* If you're a fan, this place will be a real exciter: they're not so much a theme as an object of insane devotion. The music policy is… well, you can guess. The band popped in for a beer during a tour in 2001; the regulars are probably still talking about it.

Gloria Veinikelder, Müürivahe 2, **T** 644 8846, www.gloria.ee. *Daily 1200-2300 Map 2, K5, p253* Gloria the restaurant has one of the Baltic region's best-stocked cellars, so its maze-like next-door wine bar has a headstart on the competition. Intimate nooks and opulent rooms do it no harm at all but it's the sense of refinement, heightened by classical background music, that makes this a corking venue.

Guitar Safari, Müürivahe 22, **T** 631 3360. *Mon and Tue 1200-0100, Wed and Thu 1200-0200, Fri 1200-0300, Sat 1400-0300, Sun closed. Mon-Wed 25 EEK, Thu 35 EEK, Fri and Sat 50 EEK. Map 2, J7, p253*

Terviseks!

Saku Originaal and *A Le Coq* are the most popular local beers. The Tallinn-based Saku brewery, originally founded in 1820, produces 13 beers, mainly lagers, and has an impressive stranglehold on the market; Tartu's A Le Coq, established in 1913 to make porter for the Russian market, produces a slightly sweeter lager and a smooth black beer. Visit www.beerguide.ee to discover more about Estonian brews.

If gin's your thing, *Saaremaa Dzinn*, made with juniper berries, has a clean, refreshing taste. In the 1930s, Estonia was listed in the *Guinness Book of Records* for producing the strongest vodka in the world (96%!). It is still popular, although these days 40% is the norm. (A good local brand is *Viru Valge*.)

Estonian wines, made of currants and berries, tend to be sweet, as does Estonia's 'champagne', the fresh, fruity *Fest*, made in the orchard town of Põltsamaa. Oft derided by locals, *Vana Tallinn* liqueur, the result of a secret recipe with 45 ingredients, has a sweet, medicinal taste, and is best, bizarrely, with ice cream. For a dash of 1930s nostalgia, try the recently revived caraway liqueur *Kristallkümmel*, which once accompanied every picnic, seaside trip and hunting outing, and is reputedly good for the digestion.

The Estonian word for cheers is 'Terviseks!', but do us all a favour and leave the inevitable jokes to the stag parties.

This informal basement bar, with photos of Jimi Hendrix plastered all over the walls, attracts ageing rockers thanks to regular live acts who know how to sing the blues. Reserve if you want a table.

Kaheksa, Vana-Posti 8, **T** 627 4770. *Mon-Thu 1200-2400, Fri and Sat 1200-0200. Map 2, K6, p253* Upmarket, orange-coloured lounge in the Sõprus Cinema complex, with spotlights, exotic tropical decor, leather sofas and a good range of cocktails, fruit smoothies and tasty Italian-style snacks. A good place to see and be seen, although it's all a bit Patrick Bateman.

Karja Kelder, Väike-Karja 1, **T** 644 1008, www.karjakelder.ee. *Sun and Mon 1100-2400, Tue and Thu 1100-0200, Fri and Sat 1100-0400. Map 2, I6, p253* The locals love this resolutely untrendy place, and it's easy to see why: booze and snacks at bargain prices, a casual atmosphere and occasional live music.

Kolumbus Krisostomus, Viru 24, **T** 56 156 924, www.kolumbus.ee. *Sun and Mon 1200-2300, Tue and Thu 1200-0100, Fri and Sat 1200-0300. Entry fee up to 50 EEK. Map 2, H8, p253* This bar offers welcome relief from the tourist throng. Again popular with locals, it's run by a local musician, so it's no surprise that the mainly Estonian bands who play here are actually worth listening to.

La Casa Del Habano, Dunkri 2, **T** 644 5647, www.havanas.ee. *Mon-Sat 1000-2400, Sun 1200-1800. Map 2, H5, p253* You don't have to like cigars to enjoy the relaxed, friendly atmosphere at *Havana House*, a stylish place to linger over cocktails and rum.

Levist Väljas, Olevimägi 12. *1500-0300, Fri-Sat 1500-0600. Map 2, E7, p252* Ignore the scraggle of teenage thrash freaks who hang around outside: this is one of the city's most relaxed hang-outs, with comfy, if broken, sofas, artfully renovated vaulting, cheap Estonian beer and a mixed, bohemian crowd. Fabulously eclectic music, too, from neo-psych through Tom Waits to Queens of the Stone Age.

Musi, Niguliste 6, **T** 644 3100. *Mon-Sat 1500-2400. Map 2, I4, p253* Romantic, cosy and relaxed venue with a colourful menu, good wines and decent snacks.

Bars and clubs

Nimega Baar (Bar with a Name), Suur-Karja 13, **T** 620 9299. *1100-0200, Fri and Sat 1100-0400. Map 2, J6, p253* An offshoot of the hugely successful *Nimeta*, over the road. Things hot up in the midnight hour, with a dancefloor at the back and DJs at weekends.

Nimeta Baar (Bar with no Name), Suur-Karja 4, **T** 641 1515, www.nimetabaar.ee. *Sun-Wed 1100-0200, Thu-Sat 1100-0400. Map 2, J6, p253* One of the first bars to open in the post-Soviet era, *Nimeta* was founded by a Scot who left town in a hurry. The truth behind his departure is top-secret, but it's fair to say he had a licence to thrill: with all-night dancing, DJs on weekends, pool, darts and a big screen for sports, this is one of Tallinn's pre-club hubs, and a magnet for expats.

Pegasus, Harju 1, **T** 631 4040, www.restoranpegasus.ee. *0800-0100, Fri 0800-0200, Sat 1000-0200. Map 2, J5, p253* White-walled *Pegasus* is one of the city's hottest bars, with excellent weekend DJs and an endless parade of beautiful people hell-bent on partying the night away.

Popular, Vana-Viru 6, **T** 641 4565, www.popular.ee. *0900-0100, Fri 0900-0400, Sat 1100-0400. Map 2, H8, p253* A bar with red and white decor, an upbeat feel and soulful house tunes.

Pub Kompressor, Rataskaevu 3, **T** 646 4210. *Sun-Thu 1100-0100, Fri and Sat 1100-0300. Map 2, H4, p253* High-ceilinged and orange-walled, this lively place attracts a youthful crowd with a mixture of cheap drinks and low-priced pancakes with which to soak them up.

St Patrick's, Suur-Karja 8, **T** 6314 801, www.patricks.ee. *1100-0200, Fri and Sat 1100-0400. Map 2, I6, p253* Lurking behind the Oirish name is a truly attractive establishment. Quieter than the city's more established expat hang-outs, so come to chill down, not warm up.

Šoti Klubi, Uus 33, **T** 641 1666. *Sun and Mon 1100-0200, Fri and Sat 1100-0400. Map 2, C8, p252* The only place in town serving haggis. The whisky menu is impressive but the real draw is the garden.

Stereo Lounge, Harju 6, **T** 631 0549, www.stereolounge.ee. *0800-0100, Fri 0800-0300, Sat 1100-0300, Sun 1100-0100. Map 2, L3, p253* The decor has long been the talk of Tallinn: institution- white, padded leather walls and furniture, and a vast, glowing bar with a fascia that's equal parts 1950s Cadillac fender and Roberts radio. It's a favourite of the pre-club crowd, with DJs at the weekends and a palpable buzz at all hours of the day. Refreshingly laid-back and unpretentious. Decent, down-to-earth food is an added attraction.

Tristan ja Isolde, Raekoja plats 1, **T** 644 0818. *0800-2300. Map 2, H5, p253* A late-night beer under the arches of the town hall is one of those magic Tallinn moments, better still if two hearts are sharing.

Valli bar, Müürivahe 14, **T** 641 8379. *Map 2, K6, p253* The mother of all bars, this hangover from the Soviet era is resolutely determined not to update its decor. The house speciality, *Milli-mallikas*, is a toxic blend of tequila, star anise and Tabasco.

Veinipööning, Viru 18, **T** 641 8631. *Mon-Thu 1600-2200, Fri and Sat 1600-0200. Map 2, H7, p253* Don't be put off by the downstairs casino. This is a delightfully rambling wine bar with candle-lit tables, curtains made of corkscrews, and old beds and sofas for lounging on. The choice of wines is modest but they're well kept and served.

Von Krahli Bar, Rataskaevu 10, **T** 626 9090, www.vonkrahl.ee. *1200-0100, Fri and Sat 1200-0300. Map 2, H4, p253* This dimly lit, unpretentious venue hosts live music and some of the trendiest parties in town. Locals mourn the fact that it's a bit more grand and grown-up than it was in the good old days but Tallinn wouldn't be the same without it.

Clubs

Club Privé, Harju 6, **T** 631 0545, www.clubprive.ee. *Wed 2000-, Fri-Sat 2300-0600. 150 EEK. Map 2, K4, p253* Run by the organizer of Tallinn's wild *Vibe* parties, this trendy venue offers some of the best music in town. There's live jazz on weekdays, with DJs from the Baltics and beyond on weekends.

Hollywood, Vana-Posti 8, **T** 627 4770, www.club-hollywood.ee. *Wed-Sat 2200-0500. Free entry with Tallinn Card, otherwise 40-120 EEK. Map 2, K6, p253* The first club to open in the Baltics and still the most unashamedly up-for-it place in Tallinn. Housed in the Sõprus Cinema, with Stalinist-era balconies and 1950s stucco work adding to the charm, it dabbles in hip-hop but the remarkably good-natured crowd seems happy with the retro weekend sounds. More offbeat are video clips of hilarious Soviet-era 'advertisements'. You'd have to be down-right miserable not to have a good time.

Venus Club, Vana-Viru 14, **T** 641 8184, www.venusclub.ee. *Wed and Thu 2200-0300, Fri and Sat 2200-0430. 50-100 EEK. Map 2, H8, p253* Disco inferno in a former fire station, with Russian techno stoking up a crowd of Russian-speaking twenty somethings.

Von Krahl (see Bars, above) hosts reggae/dancehall nights (www.bashment.ee) and hip-hop nights (www.huh.ee).

Kesklinn

Bars

Woodstock, Tatari 6, 1st floor, **T** 660 4915. *1200-0600. Map 3, I3, p255* Tallinn was not exactly swinging in the 1960s, but this place celebrates the era with a retro feel: comfy sofas, bean bags, a small dancefloor and a mixed, unpretentious local crowd.

Clubs

Café Amigo, Viru väljak 4, **T** 680 9300, www.viru.ee. *2100-0400, Fri-Sat 2100-0500. Sun-Wed 60 EEK, Thu-Sat 100 EEK. Map 3, F6, p254* Relaxed atmosphere where thirty-somethings feel at home.

Moskva, Vabaduse väljak10, **T** 640 46 94, www.moskva.ee. *Café and restaurant 0900-2400, Sat and Sun 1100-2400. Map 3, G2, p255* The downstairs café is one of Tallinn's prime posing points, but it's less intimidating than it looks from the outside. Shake your stuff to uplifting house tunes on the compact dancefloor.

Nightman, Vineeri 4, www.nightman.ee. *Fri and Sat 2300-0600, not worth arriving before 0100. Map 1, F6, p250* Originally a gay club, Nightman gets pretty wild in the wee small hours, the atmosphere fuelled by crowd-pleasing house and soul grooves. A taxi ride away from the Old Town via Pärnu maantee.

Sossi Klubi, Tartu maantee 82, **T** 601 4384, www.sossi.ee. *Wed 2000-0100, Thu-Sat 2000-0300, closed Sun-Wed. 60-100 EEK. Map 1, F8, p251* If you feel out of place at teenage techno haunts, try this friendly club, where a mature crowd comes to life without inhibitions for easy-going jazz, blues and rock sounds.

Võit (Victory), Tatari 64, www.lovesexmoney.ee. *Map 3, J4, p255* A low-key underground venue hosting techno, drum 'n' base and rock nights.

Harbour and around

Bars

Scotland Yard, Mere puiestee 6e, **T** 653 5190, www.scotland
yard.ee. *Sun-Wed 0900-2400, Thu-Sat 0900-0300. Map 3, D6, p254*
Housed in the Rotermanni industrial complex, this prodigiously large
pub is gimmicky – fake bookshelves, suits of armour, waiters and
waitresses dressed as London bobbies – but the Englishness evoked
by the name has won the hearts of many locals. There's often live
music, and it's the kind of pub where people end up dancing.

Clubs

Bon Bon, Mere puiestee 6e, **T** 661 60 80, www.bonbon.ee. *Wed,
Fri, Sat 2200 till late. Map 3, C6, p254* The only place in Tallinn
where you're likely to hear bhangra, as well as global grooves,
house, Asian hip-hop, jazz and 1970s hits.

Parlament, Tartu maantee 17, **T** 666 2900, www.club
parlament.com. *Map 3, G8, p255* House, techno and R&B in a vast
venue that attracts a young crowd.

Terrarium, Sadama 6, **T** 661 4721, www.terrarium.ee. *Wed-Sat
2200-0400. Wed-Thu 50 EEK, Fri-Sat 100 EEK. Map 3, A6, p254* This
vast place near the port has a huge, and usually rammed, dancefloor
connected to the people-watching gallery by a monumental curved
staircase. Commercial dance music, a disco night and cheap drinks.

Kalamaja and Kopli Bay

Ilmataar, Kopli 6, **T** 641 5337. *Map 1, D5, p250* Russian karaoke
bar near the Balti jaam. A world unto itself, where vodka drinking is

de rigueur, the dancing is wild, lonesome males buy every woman in the club a bunch of red roses and even the shyest are somehow persuaded to take the microphone.

Nõmme

Buldogi Pub, Jaama 2, **T** 650 4123, www.buldogipub.ee. *Sun-Thu 1100-2400, Fri and Sat 1100-0200. Map 1, I3, p250* On Nõmme's main square, this is the most popular pub in the suburb. A good place to meet the locals and enjoy a game of billiards.

Pärnu

Bars

Pärnu Kuursaal, Mere puiestee 22, **T** 44 40367, www.kuur.ee. *Sun-Thu 1200-0200, Fri and Sat 1200-0400*. A vast, fun and lively tavern with live bands playing anything from covers to Estonian folk.

Veerev Õlu, Uus 3a-2, **T** 44 29848. *1100-0100, Sun 1300-0100*. Friendly, rustic-style pub with an attractive courtyard.

Clubs

Club Tallinn, Kuursaal (see above), www.clubtallinn.ee. *Tue-Sat 2200-0400 in summer, closed Sun-Mon*. Tartu's hugely successful club wisely moves to Pärnu in summer, as do most of the students. Without question the summer capital's trendiest venue.

Sunset Club, Ranna puiestee 3, **T** 44 30670, www.sunsetclub.ee. *Fri 2100-0300, Sat 2100-0300, open year-round, best in summer*. Sun, sea and summer sounds, with live bands and DJs inside the building and on a stage by the sea. Crazy nights guaranteed.

Tartu

Bars

Illegaard, Ülikooli 5, **T** 742 3443. *Mon-Thu 1200-0200, Fri 1200-0300, Sat 1900-0200. 30-35 EEK.* A jazz café frequented by musicians, actors and writers.

Krooks, Jakobi 34, **T** 744 1506. *Daily 1200-0400.* Owned by a musician, this is a great late-night pub with a good selection of beer.

Tsink Plekk Pang, Küütri 6, **T** 744 1789, www.tsinkplekkpang.ee, *Tue-Sat 1200-2400, Sun and Mon 1200-2300.* Hugely popular Chinese restaurant-cum-venue. DJs on Friday and Saturday nights and occasional parties, including Jazzitup, organised by Peovool.

Zum-Zum, Küüni 2, **T** 744 1438. *Mon-Thu 1100-2400, Fri 1100-0100, Sat 1000-0100, Sun 1000-2300.* Central pub, just off Raekoja plats, that shows televised football matches.

Clubs

Atlantis, Narva maantee 2, **T** 738 5484, www.atlantis.ee. *Thu-Sat 2200-0400.* Riverside club popular with students in search of disco music.

Club Tallinn, Narva maantee 27, **T** 740 3157, www.clubtallinn.ee. *Fri and Sat 2200-0400.* A popular student venue and one of Estonia's trendiest clubs. The emphasis is on house, jazz and acid jazz.

Club XS, Vaksali 21, **T** 730 3640, www.xs.ee. *Tue-Thu 2200-0300, Fri and Sat 2200-0400.* Popular with the late teens and early twenties party crowd.

Estonians are avid consumers of culture, and plays, concerts and dance performances regularly sell out. It's worth trying to get tickets, though, because many events are staged in beautiful historic venues worth a visit in themselves.

For a small country, Estonia has produced a remarkable number of world-renowned conductors and composers – Arvo Pärt is the most famous – and the level of musicianship is extremely high. Contemporary dance is also thriving. Mainstream American films take up much of the cinema programme, but there is strong support for local and European films and animation.

Tallinn winds down in the summer, when seaside Pärnu takes over as 'summer capital', although affordable concerts and open-air plays are on offer throughout the summer. Daily events are advertised in the national newspapers and the tourist office. Posters detailing monthly events are found throughout Tallinn; there's one on Saiakang, just off Raekoja plats. See also www.tourism.tallinn.ee and www.culture.ee, both in English.

Cinema

The Estonian film industry is small and, since the collapse of planned film production in 1989 and the lifting of state censorship in 1990, there have been huge changes in style, content and financing. Producers have had to find new ways of raising funds, often via foreign partners. *Darkness in Tallinn* (1993), a tale of local thieves stealing gold reserves being returned to the newly independent Estonia, was a Finnish venture that found favour in the West.

Estonia's answer to Darryl Zanuck is media mogul Kristian Taska (his father, Ilmar, was a Hollywood producer), who scored a big hit at home with *Names in Marble* (2002, directed by Elmo Nüganen), about a class of ill-equipped schoolboys who fought in Estonia's Independence War. *Revolution of the Pigs* (2004, directed by Jaak Klimi and Rene Reinumagi), is about life in Soviet summer camps and won the Jury Special prize in Moscow. Tallinn University is to open a media and film school for the Baltic states.

Estonian animation, much of it absurdist and darkly comic, has bagged a staggering number of animation festival awards. The internationally acclaimed Priit Pärn's best works include *Lunch on the Grass* (1987), about a poet in a totalitarian world, and *Hotel E* (1992), about the integration of Europe. Another Soviet-era classic is Rein Raamat's *Hell*, based on drawings by Eduard Viiralt.

There are three main cinemas in Tallinn, all showing largely US films in English, with Estonian subtitles. **Coca-Cola Plaza Multiplex** (Hobujaama 5, **T** 1182, www.mpde.ee *Map 3, E6, p254*) is the most high-tech with 11 screens. **Kosmos** (Pärnu maantee 45, **T** 1182, www.superkinod.ee *Map 3, K2, p255*) was the city's largest cinema in Soviet times but is now rather dated. **Sõprus** (Vana-Posti 8, **T** 644 1919, www.kino.ee *Map 2, J5, p253*) is housed in a pompous neoclassical Stalinist building in the Old Town. Tallinn's one atmospheric arthouse cinema screens retrospectives: **Eesti Kino-liit Kinomaja** (Uus 3, **T** 646 4164, www.kinoliit.ee *Map 2, G8, p253*)

Dance

Estonia has a strong folk-dancing tradition, often humorous, but rarely spectacular. Catch a performance at a song festival or on summer weekends at the Rocca al Mare open-air museum (see p87). The Estonian National Ballet has a varied and creative repertoire. Look out for dancers Marina Chirkova, Vladimir Arhagenslki and Linnar Looris.

Modern dance in Estonia has surprisingly deep roots, and Tallinn audiences are very receptive to new work. The biggest event in the contemporary calendar is August's Dance Festival, which attracts big names from abroad. With top tickets priced at 120 EEK, all the performances are sellouts. Local dancers/choreographers to look out for include Mart Kangro, Renate Keerd and Katrin Essenson, while the two biggest troupes are *Fine 5 Dance Theatre* and *2.Tants*. If you want to know more, visit www.criticaldance.com.

Estonia National Opera, Estonia puiestee 4, **T** 683 1260, www.opera.ee.   *Map 2, K8, p253* Sumptuous cream-and-yellow venue hosting opera and ballet performances.

Kanuti Gildi Saal, Pikk 20, **T** 646 4704, www.saal.ee. *Map 2, G5, p253* Impressive, recently spruced-up historicist hall, the home of contemporary dance in Tallinn. Bohemian atmosphere.

Von Krahl, Rataskaevu 10, **T** 626 9090, www.vonkrahl.ee. *Map 2, H4, p253* Tallinn's oldest theatre hosts occasional avant-garde performances.

Music

As you'd expect in a country that gained independence through the Singing Revolution, music is hugely important in Estonia. During the Soviet era, when there was almost no nightlife and songs were subject to censorship, there was a flourishing underground rock scene. Come the revolution, however, Europop arrived and, for a country that had missed out on disco, the temptation of techno, techno, techno, techno proved too great.

Aruban-born Dave Benton, of Eurovision fame (he and national hero Tanel Padar won the event for Estonia in 2002), has the best band name in town, King of Spades. Unreconstructed rockers should look out for Smilers, primal-screamer Peeter Volkonski, Eesti Keeled's acoustica and Ultima Thule. Progressive punks Vennaskond are Estonia's answer to Muse. Blues and folk are also flourishing.

During the Soviet era, when jazz was a prohibited expression of western decadence, Tallinn was one of the few places in the Soviet Union where you could hear anything like it. Today, Tallinn hosts a spring jazz festival (Jazzkaar). The best local band are the Weekend Guitar Trio, with Jaak Sooäär and saxophonist Raivo Tafenau.

While Estonian pop has hit a rocky patch, its classical musicians are blooming. Arvo Pärt, who fled the country with his family in 1980 and eventually settled in Germany, is one of the few living composers anyone has heard of. His haunting *Cantus in memoriam Benjamin Britten* has provided instant atmosphere in scores of BBC Radio 4 dramas, and was used by Michael Moore in *Fahrenheit 9/11*. Other contemporary composers to look out for include Veljo Tormis (folk song meets avant-garde), former rock musician Erki Sven Tüür, and Helena Tulve.

Ensembles to look out for include Hortus Musicus, whose spirited renditions of early music are a feast for the eye as well as the ear. The innovative NYYD ('nude') ensemble performs works by the likes of Louis Andriessen, John Adams and Michael Nyman, as well as up-and-coming Estonian composers.

Don't miss concerts by Estonia's national choirs (such as the Ellerhein Girls' Choir), world- renowned Estonian conductors Eri Klas, Neeme Järvi and son, Paavo Järvi, or the Estonian Philharmonic Chamber choir. For information about Estonian music, consult www.emic.kul.ee, which has information in English.

Vox pop
The Estonian National Opera is at the heart of Tallinn's flourishing cultural life.

Classical and opera

The Estonia Opera has room for both moderate novelty (works by Orff, Britten and contemporary Estonian composers Eino Tamberg, René Eespere, Timo Steineri and Rimo Kangro) and tradition (Verdi, Mussorgsky and so on). Singers to look out for include the long established Mati Palm and Teo Meister (bass), sopranos Riina Airenne, Nadja Kurem and Pille Lill, tenor Mati Kõrts, baritone Jassi Zahharov and bass Leonid Savistski. There are only occasional performances from visiting companies. The opera is also home to the Estonian ballet. From mid-May to September, the opera is closed and performances tour the country. For details of classical music concerts, see www.eestikontsert.ee. From the UK you can book tickets on on www.operasabroad.com or **T** 0151 493 0382.

Estonia Concert Hall, Estonia puiestee 4, **T** 614 7700. *Map 2, K9, p253* This beautifully renovated venue is the city's finest auditorium. It also houses **Eesti Kontsert**, which promotes concerts nationwide, **T** 614 7760, www.concert.ee. *Ticket office Mon-Fri 1200-1900, Sat 1200-1700.*

Sound and silence

Arvo Pärt's starkly beautiful blend of old and new has captivated audiences everywhere. Influenced by everything from medieval and Gregorian chant to minimalism, he has experimented with polytonality, collage, pointillism and pastiche. The technique he is most often associated with is 'tintinnabuli', a mixture of almost static repetition and constantly moving sounds that can be likened to the ringing of bells. The result is deceptively simple, deeply harmonious, melodic and mystical. In his own words: "I have discovered that it is enough when a single note is beautifully played. This one note, or a silent beat, or a moment of silence, comforts me. I work with very few elements – with one voice, two voices. I build with primitive materials – with the triad, with one specific tonality. The three notes of a triad are like bells and that is why I call it tintinnabulation."

His best-known works include *Fratres*, *Passio* and *Tabula Rasa*, and his contribution to contemporary music was recognized with his election to the American Academy of Arts aged 61.

For those who were 'lucky' enough to be there, the most memorable Pärt performance took place in 1977, at the peak of Soviet stagnation, when the Latvian-born violinist Gidon Kremer performed the emotionally charged première of Pärt's hauntingly sparse *Tabula Rasa* in Tallinn. As Kremer told me in 1997: "The piece was a declaration of silence and of the need to concentrate on important issues."

Pärt is an elusive, even reclusive, figure who rarely gives interviews or explains his work, but a good starting point is the biography written by British conductor Paul Hillier, an early-music pioneer who has premiered many of the composer's vocal works (see Books, p234).

★ **Free concert venues (classical music)**

Best

- Toomkirik, p40
- Stenbock House courtyard, p41
- Pühavaimu, p61
- Kaarli Kirik, p67
- Niguliste, p182

Lauluväljak (Song Grounds), Narva maantee 95, **T** 611 2102, www.lauluvaljak.ee. *Map 1, D9, p251* This vast stage and grounds host the national Song Festival, plus pop, rock and classical events.

Methodist Church, Narva maantee 51, **T** 668 8460, www.metodist kirik.ee. *Detail map, G9, p250* World-class concerts, great acoustics.

Mustpeade Maja, Pikk 26, **T/F** 631 3199, www.mustpeademaja.ee. *Map 2, G5, p253* This 15th-century guildhall hosts regular concerts.

Niguliste Museum-Concert Hall, Niguliste 3, **T** 644 9911, www.ekm.ee/english/niguliste. *Map 2, I4, p253* Organ recitals, choral concerts and soloists in a 13th-century Gothic church.

Pirita Klooster, Merivälja tee 18, **T** 605 5044, www.piritaklooster.ee. *Map 1, B10, p251* Open-air summer concerts, both popular and classical.

Tallinn Town Hall, Raekoja plats 1, **T** 645 7900, www.tallinn.ee /raekoda. *Map 2, H5, p253* Classical concerts in a perfect setting.

Väravatorn, Lühike jalg 9, **T** 644 0719, www.concert.ee. *Map 2, J3, p253* This intimate venue in a medieval tower is home to the Hortus Musicus ensemble.

Arts and entertainment

Rock and pop

City Concert Hall (Linnahall), Mere puiestee 20, **T** 641 2250, www.linnahall.ee *Map 1, D6, p250* Huge, ugly grey structure by the harbour, home to pop concerts and musicals.

Guitar Safari, Müürivahe 22, **T** 627 0186, www.megainfo.ee *Map 2, J7, p253* Basement venue hidden away on a narrow Old Town street. Attracts a mixed-age audience hungry for blues and rock.

Kolumbus Krisostomus, Viru 2, **T** 056 156 924, www.kolumbus.ee. *Map 2, H8, p253* Relaxed, airy second-floor venue a stone's throw from Viru Gate, with good local bands.

Saku Suurhall, Paldiski maantee 14b, **T** 660 0216, www.saku suurhall.ee. *Map 1, E1, p250* Concerts and sporting events are held at this giant venue, built to host the 2002 Eurovision Song Contest.

Von Krahl, Rataskaevu 10, **T** 626 9090, www.vonkrahl.ee. *Map 2, H4, p253* Appealing venue for Estonian rock and blues bands, with an arty atmosphere and an upstairs gallery.

Theatre

Theatre in Tallinn is thriving. There are many wonderful venues and musical productions can easily be appreciated by non-Estonian speakers. The current scene is fairly conservative, with contemporary Estonia and the Estonian character popular themes. In the Soviet era, playwrights subtly tackled topics that could not be openly discussed, and theatregoers got their kicks by looking for hidden messages. Today's audiences, however, are understandably more interested in escapist entertainment.

Eesti Draamateater (Estonian Drama Theatre), Pärnu maantee 5, **T** 681 5555, www.dramateater.ee. *Closed in August.* *Map 3, G4, p255* A Jugendstil theatre built in 1910 as the German Theatre. The repertoire spans Shakespeare, Molière and Friel, as well as Estonian classics and works by local dramatists, including Madis Kõiv.

Eesti Nukuteater (Estonian Puppet Theatre), Lai 1, **T** 667 9550, www.nukuteater.ee. *Map 2, G4, p253* This cosy venue puts on plays for children and young people: rock musicals, revues and puppet shows. Summer performances take place in the yard.

Linnateater (Tallinn City Theatre), Lai 23, **T** 665 0850, www.linna teater.ee. *Map 2, D5, p252* Housed in several medieval houses and much bigger than it looks from the street. The programme ranges from Russian classics to contemporary Swedish plays, mostly tackled in a naturalistic style. Tickets cost around 200 EEK.

Salong-Teater (Salon Theatre), Kaarli puiestee 9, **T** 645 3875, www.salong-teater.ee. *Map 3, H1, p255* A private, intimate 50-seater venue. Repertory mainstays include avant-garde versions of Molière, Shakespeare, Pushkin, Boccaccio and Chekhov.

Vanalinna Stuudio (Old Town Studio), Sakala 3, **T** 668 8798, www.vanalinnastuudio.ee. *Map 3, H5, p255* Modern classics by dramatists from around the world.

Vene Draamateater (Russian Drama Theatre), Vabaduse väljak 5, **T** 641 8246, www.grdt.ee. *Map 2, L5, p253* Classic repertory theatre with Russian and western drama by the likes of Calderon, Chekhov, Ostrovsky, Razumovsky and Dostoevsky.

Von Krahl, Rataskaevu 10, **T** 626 9090, www.vonkrahl.ee. *Map 2, H4, p253* Tallinn's most experimental theatre uses modern technology and spans opera and non-Estonian works in translation.

Traditional celebrations are still a vital part of life in Estonia, especially in summer, when those who can rush to rural parts to celebrate midsummer. The three-day country wedding may be a rarity these days, but singing, which has always been connected with national identity, remains hugely popular, be it drunkenly around a midsummer fire or at one of the many song festivals. Today, the national song and dance festival is still a huge event, although it has, thankfully, lost its political urgency. Classical and contemporary music festivals are usually excellent and top-price tickets are rarely more than 300 EEK. In summer, a host of festivals take place outside the capital, especially in Pärnu. Pretty much anything is celebrated, from home-made wine to bagpipe-playing and woman-carrying.

February

Baroque Music Days (early Feb). Week-long early-music event, run by the charismatic director of Hortus Musicus, Andrus Mustonen.

April

Jazzkaar (end Apr). Best translated as 'Rainbow of Jazz', this top-notch week-long festival, staged in Tallinn, Tartu, Pärnu and Haapsalu, includes a piano marathon and a vocal day. Past guests include Richard Galliano and Jan Garbarek.

May

Day of Tallinn (15th). On this day in 1248, the King of Denmark gave Tallinn the rights of Lübeck, allowing it to enter the Hanseatic League.

International Choir Contest, Pärnu (late May; next event in 2007). A triennial celebration of choral excellence.

June

Old Town Days (1st weekend). The beginning of summer is celebrated with handicrafts, concerts, folk dancing, exhibitions and street shows, some from abroad and most of them free.

Baltica International Folklore Festival (mid-Jun). This rambunctious revel rotates between Estonia, Latvia and Lithuania.

Midsummer (23rd-24th). Bonfires are lit across the country in honour of St John's Night, then the drinking starts. Grillfest, a group supporting old traditions, organizes the biggest party, www.grillfest.ee.

David Oistrakh Festival, Pärnu (end Jun-mid Jul). Taking its name from the prodigious Russian violinist, this prestigious classical music festival pulls in top players such as Gidon Kremer.

July

Estonian Song Festival (2nd-4th; the next event is in 2008). The nation's biggest song festival is held every four years in the vast Song Festival Grounds. The stage holds up to 25,000 singers, and the 1988 event helped spark the Singing Revolution.

Õllesummer Festival (Beer Summer Festival) (early Jul). The main attraction speaks for itself, but this family-friendly, five-day event in the Song Festival Grounds also offers a chance to see classical, pop, folk and jazz concerts and fireworks. Free with Tallinn Card.

International Documentary and Anthropology Film Festival, Pärnu. The country's best showcase for documentary film, with retrospectives, obscure but enlightening films about folklore and rituals from around the world, new Estonian documentaries and children's films.

Art Summer Pärnu. As the name suggests, a season of exhibitions, centred on the New Art Museum (see p114).

August

International Organ Festival (early Aug). A world-class event, staged in Tallinn, Tartu and Pärnu, with top organists only too happy to reap the benefits of Estonia's renovation programme.

August Dance Festival (late Aug). Cutting-edge modern dance festival at Tallinn's Kanuti Guildi Saal, www.saal.ee. Whether the

▶ Singing for freedom

The first Song Festival was held in Tartu, heart of the country's National Awakening, in 1869, to celebrate the abolition of serfdom. One of its founders was the poetess Lydia Koidula, whose patriotic poems were set to exuberant music. Singing in Estonia has always been connected with resistance to oppression, most obviously in the Singing Revolution of the late 1980s, which involved regular get-togethers in the Song Festival Grounds and the singing of forbidden songs. Although the Soviet administration allowed Estonians to run the festivals, they were picky about their content and tried to use them as an expression of support for the regime. The 1988 festival was a hugely emotive event that attracted 300,000 people. Today, the song festival has lost its urgent political edge, but it is still an important cultural event, and the quality of the performances has, if anything, improved. Although many locals were initially blasé about 2004's event, it still proved to be a special occasion, attracting even the trendiest of Estonians.

performances are by local troupes or international names, tickets are snapped up at lightning pace by Tallinn's avid dance fans.

Bagpipe Festival, Lahemaa (every two years, next in 2007). Part of the Baltica Folklore Festival; info from Estonian National Folklore Council, **T** 644 2927, anne.ojalo@kul.ee.

September

Credo International Festival of Sacred Music (end Sep). Top-quality celebration of church music.

Print Triennial, Rotermann Salt Storage, Tallinn (Sep-Oct; next event in 2007). Graphic art and prints. www.triennial.ee.

October

NYYD Festival (late Oct-early Nov). A superb new-music festival devoted to the likes of Gavin Bryars, Steve Reich, Gyorgy Ligeti and Finland's Esa-Pekka Salonen, as well as local hero Erkki Sven-Tuur and a host of new and electronic sounds.

November

St Martin's Day Fair (beginning Nov), www.folkart.ee. Handicraft stalls, workshops, food stalls, folk music and Martinmas costumes in the Song Festival Grounds.

Black Nights Film Festival (PÖFF) (late Nov-early Dec). Two-week showcase for world feature films of the past two years, with an emphasis on European and Estonian film. In competition: animated shorts, student films and films for children.

Christmas Jazz, www.jazzkaar.ee (late Nov-early Dec). Three-week jazz extravaganza, by the same people as the April Jazzkaar (see above).

December

Midwinter Night's Dream (every two years; 27-31 Dec 2006). Companies from Scandinavia, Russia, Germany and even Southeast Asia congregate every two years for a feast of avant-garde theatre in Tallinn.

Visiting Tallinn today, it doesn't seem possible that only 15 years ago you had to queue for overpriced, over-ripe tomatoes, or make do without toothpaste and toilet paper. Now the Old Town is awash with souvenir shops selling everything from amber and Russian dolls to linen tops, wrought-iron candelabras, juniper-wood butter knives and impossibly thick, folksy winter socks. Viru tänav is the main shopping street. There are regular handicraft markets on Raekoja plats, particularly atmospheric during June's Old Town Days and at Christmas. Antiques shops sell everything from (hopefully) authentic icons to Soviet army medals and pre-war toys. It's also worth checking out Estonian designer clothes. Large supermarkets and shopping malls have sprung up everywhere in the past decade, most near the port or on the roads out of town. Off-licences are equally ubiquitous, and cheap. Most shops accept major credit and debit cards, and are generally open from 0900 or 1000 to 1800 or 1900, although larger supermarkets are open longer and on Sundays. There are several 24-hour shops.

Antiques

Caveat emptor: unless you are an expert, it's hard to get any guarantee that what you are buying is genuine, even if it comes with a certificate of authenticity. Many 'antiques' shops have more in common with bric-a-brac stores. The following are at the top end:

Antiik, Vanaturu kael 10/12, **T** 641 8050. *Map 2, H6, p253*
Upmarket antiques, especially Russian silver.

Jaanus Idla Antiik, Pikk 43, **T** 646 4060. *Mon-Fri 1000-1800, Sat 1000-1700. Map 2, E6, p252* Russian Orthodox icons.

Raeantiik, Raekoja plats 11, **T** 644 2639. *Mon-Fri 1000-1900, Sat 1000-1700. Map 2, G7, p253* Soviet memorabilia, 1930s toys.

Reval Antiik, Pikk 31, **T** 644 0747. *Mon-Sat 1000-1800. Map 2, F6, p252* Photographs, postcards, lamps.

Art

Draakoni Galerii, Pikk 18, **T** 646 4110. *Mon-Fri 1000-1800, Sat and Sun 1000-1700. Map 2, G5, p252* Housed in a stunning Jugendstil building, this gallery sells Estonian art and hosts exhibitions.

Haus Gallery, Uus 17, **T** 641 9471, www.haus.ee. *Mon-Fri 1000-1800, Sat 1100-1600. Map 2, E8, p252* Tallinn's best by a mile, with a well-selected collection of paintings by Estonia's biggest names and graphic works to browse.

Vaal Gallery, Tartu maantee 80, **T** 699 6401, www.vaal.ee. *Mon-Fri 1100-1800, Sat 1100-1600. Map 1, F7, p251* Private commercial gallery. Excellent displays of contemporary Estonian and foreign art.

Bookshops

Allecto, Juhkentali 8, **T** 627 7230, www.allecto.ee. *Mon-Fri 0900-1800, Sat 1100-1600.* Foreign language books, fiction and children's literature.

Antikvariaat, Uus 11, **T** 648 4318. *Mon-Fri 1000-1800, Sat 1000-1500. Map 2, F8, p252* High-quality old maps and books.

Apollo Raamatumaja, Viru 23, **T** 654 8485, www.apollo.ee. *Map 2, H8, p253* Well-stocked shop with an internet café and a host of books in English.

Mr Kolk, 28/30 Rüütli, **T** 641 8005, 631 4719. *Map 2, K3, p253* Eccentric, impossibly narrow second-hand bookshop overflowing with old magazines and books.

Raamatupood A & O, Narva maantee 4, **T** 699 9649, www.ene.ee. *Mon-Fri 0900-1900, Sat 0900-1500. Map 3,E8, p254* Encyclopaedias, reference books, maps and dictionaries.

Rahva Raamat, Pärnu maantee 10, **T** 644 3682. *Mon-Fri 0900-2000, Sat 1000-1700, Sun 1000-1600. Map 3, I3, p255* Excellent selection of books about Estonia.

Department stores

Kaubamaja, Gonsiori 2, **T** 667 3100, www.kaubamaja.ee. *Mon-Sat 0900-2100, Sun 1000-1900. Map 2, H6 p253* Decent range of smart and casual clothes, with clubbing gear on the top floor along with good toy department and a decent food hall. In Soviet times, it was the city's sole department store.

Shopping

Stockmann, Liivalaia 53, **T** 633 9500,
www.stockmann.ee. *Mon-Fri 0900-2100, Sat and Sun
0900-2000. Map 3, H8 p255* This Finnish department store set new
standards for choice and product quality when it opened. Good for
Western fashion, food and drink.

Fashion

Bastion, Viru 12, **T** 644 1555, www.bastion.ee. *Mon-Fri 1000- 1900,
Sat 1100-1800, Sun 1100-1600. Map 2, H7 p253* Smart casuals.

Ivo Nikkolo, Suur-Karja 14, **T** 644 4834, www.ivonikkolo.com.
*Mon-Fri 1000-1900, Sat 1000-1700, Sun 1000-1600. Map 2, J6
p253* Estonia's best-known designer makes classic, eminently
wearable clothes with a contemporary twist for men and women.

Kairi Vilderson, Aia 3, WW Passaz, **T** 627 1210. *Mon-Sat 1000-
2000, Sun 1000-1700. Map 2, H9 p253* Smart casual clothes for
women.

Nu Nordik, Vabaduse väljak 8, **T/F** 644 9392, www.nunordik.ee.
Mon-Fri 1000-1800, Sat 1100-1800. Map 2, L5 p253 By far the most
interesting designer shop in town. Besides clothes, you'll find hats,
jewellery, clocks, home furnishings and cutting-edge CDs, all by
local designers.

Pif-Paf Shop, Vana-Viru 6, www.pifpaf.ee. *Mon-Sat 1000 1900,
Sun 1000-1700. Map 2, H8 p253* Trendy shop with a good
selection of clubbing gear and skatewear.

Food

The best food halls in town are at the Stockmann and Kaubamaja
department stores (see above).

Bonaparte (see Eating, p146) *Map 2, E6, p252* Excellent takeaway croissants, cakes and quiches.

Bonaparte Deli (see above). *Mon-Sat 1000-1800.* Sells superb cakes, savoury snacks and various flavours of ice cream, including basil.

Boulevard, Hotel Olümpia, Liivalaia 33, **T** 631 5333, *Map 3, J7 p255* Cakes and pastries.

City Market *Map 3, C8 p254* Large supermarket near the port, with a good fish counter.

Kolmjalg, Pikk 3, **T** 631 1511. *Map 2, G4, p253* 24-hour store, also sells alcohol.

Mademoiselle Café, Grand Hotel Tallinn, Toompuistee 27. *Map 1, D5, p250* Fresh cakes and pastries, half price during happy hour (2100-2200).

Handicrafts and applied art

Elderly ladies sell machine-made and hand-knitted goods on the so-called 'Wall of Sweaters' along Müürivahe, *0900-1700*. The walkway next to the Great Guild that connects Pikk and Lai streets is lined with stalls selling applied art of varying quality; note that most prices here are in euros, not kroons.

A-Galerii, Hobusepea 2, **T** 646 4101. *Mon-Fri 1000-1800, Sat 1100-1600. Map 2, F5, p252* Exhibitions and sale of one off works by Estonia's best jewellery designers.

The Estonian Folk Art and Craft Union (Kodukäsitöö), **T** 660 4772, www.crafts.ee. *Map 2, I6, p253* Several outlets where you can be sure of finding genuine Estonian handicrafts, including knitwear, textiles, carved wooden items and dolls. Try Pikk 11, *1000-1800*; Müürivahe 17, *Mon-Fri 0900-1700, Sat 0900-1800*; Kuninga 1, *Mon-Sat 1000-1800*; or the branch at Viru 1, Demini Kaubamaja, *Mon-Sat 1000-1900, Sun 1100-1700*.

Galerii Kaks, Lühike jalg 1, **T/F** 641 8308. *Mon-Sat 1000-1800, Sun 1000-1700. Map 2, I3, p253* Especially good for glassware and jewellery, with pieces by artists whose work is on show in the Applied Art Museum.

Helina Tilk, Lühike jalg 5, **T** 631 3328. *Mon-Fri 0900-1800, Sat 1000-1700, Sun 1000-1500. Map 2, I3, p253* Hand-painted plates, mugs and other kitchenware, aprons, tablecloths and pillows.

Keraamika Ateljee, Pikk 33, **T** 646 4096, www.hot.ee/ asuurkeraamika. *Mon-Fri 1000-1800, Sat 1200-1700. Map 2, E6, p252* Weird, wonderful and not very practical ceramics.

Puupood, Lai 5, **T** 641 2473. *Mon-Fri 1030-1900, Sat and Sun 1000-1700. Map 2, F4 p252* Artisanal woodcarvings.

Sepa Äri, Vanaturu kael 3. *Mon-Fri 1100-1800, Sat 1100-1700. Map 2, H6 p253* Wrought iron, jewellery, traditional Estonian brooches.

Suveniir, Dunkri 2, **T** 644 4816. *1000-1800. Map 2, H5 p253* Small store with a good choice of wooden toys, including windmills.

Zizi, Vene 12, **T** 644 1222. *Mon-Sat 1000-1800, Sun 1000-1600. Map 2, G7 p253* Trendy design store selling linen, fabrics and furnishings.

Markets

Keskturg (Central Market), Keldrimäe 9, **T** 660 6304. *Daily 0800-1800. Map 3, I9 p255* Lively fruit, vegetable, flower and just about anything else market.

Music

Do-Re-Mi, Nunne tänav 1, **T/F** 644 0480. *Mon-Fri 0930-1800, Sat 0930-1700. Map 2, G4 p253* Charmingly old-fashioned, website-free shop selling jazz, classical and contemporary Estonian CDs and sheet music for works by Estonian composers.

Lasering, www.lasering.ee, *Map 3, J2, p255* The leading CD retailer, and sells a good range of Estonian music. Branches to be found all over Tallinn.

Off-licences and wine shops

Citymarket has a good, inexpensive selection, while **Kaubamaja** and **Stockmann** both have well-stocked liquor sections. For the best wines, try **Vinoteek**, Niguliste 6, **T** 631 3891, *Map 2, I4 p253*, or **Gloria**, p165, both of which are also attractive wine bars.

Shopping centres

De la Gardie, Viru 13/15, **T** 631 4754, www.delagardie.ee. *1000-2000. Map 2, H7-8 p253* High-street fashion and cosmetics.

Melon, Estonia puiestee 1. *Mon-Sat 1000-2000, Sun 1000-1800. Map 3, F6 p254* Youth fashion and shoes.

Viru Keskus, Viru väljak 4, **T** 610 1444. *Daily 0800-2200. Map 3, E6, p254* Sells everything under the sun.

Tallinn has decent facilities for most sports and leisure activities, but its best asset by far is the countryside that surrounds it. In summer, hiking and cycling are the main attractions, while in winter, the flat landscape lends itself to cross-country skiing. Although football is the main spectator sport, the standard is low by European standards; one game that's always worth catching, however, as much for the camaraderie of the fans as the quality of the action, is a match between Estonia and Scotland. The teams have clashed frequently in World and European Cup qualifiers over the past decade, most famously in 1998, when a late change of venue meant the Estonian side couldn't reach the stadium in time. The Scots won the match, but Tallinn won the Tartan Army's heart.

Outside football, the first Estonian Olympic gold medal went to Kristjan Palusalu for both freestyle and classical wrestling in 1936. Crowds greeted him at the station on his return and the state rewarded him with a farm. Visit www.seikleja.com for adventure sports, such as winter trip-skating.

Athletics

Tallinn Sports Hall, Staadioni 8/Herne 30, **T** 646 6346, www.tsh.ee.
*Map 1, F6, p250 Sep-May Mon-Fri 0800-2200, Sat and Sun 1000-1900;
Jun-Aug Mon-Fri 1200-2100, Sat 1000-1900, Sun closed.*

Boating (Pirita River Valley)

Barrel BG Boats, Kloostri 6a, opposite the Olympic complex,
T 632 1779, www.barrelbg.ee. Rowboat 75 EEK per hour
1000-1200, 100 EEK 1200-2200; pedalo 50-60 EEK per hour. Free
boat trips with Tallinn Card. Photo ID required as deposit.

Canoeing

Lahemaa Trip Centre (Lahemaa Matkakeskus), **T** 509 3177,
www.lahemaa.info. Canoe trips on the rivers Loobu and Valgejõgi.

Golf

Visit www.golf.ee for information.

Gyms

Club 26, Reval Hotel Olümpia, Liivalaia 33, **T** 631 5585. *Daily
1830-2300. Map 3, J7, p255* Superb views from the 26th floor.

Fitnessclub, Regati puiestee 1, **T** 639 6707, www.fitnessclub.ee.
Map 1, B9, p251

! Paul Keres, Estonia's celebrated chess champion, was forced to
make losing moves in the 1948 World Chess Championship.
Russian Mikhail Botvinnik won after the Soviets told Keres to
lose or risk being deported to Siberia with his family.

▶ Working up a sweat

Not for the pregnant, the pissed or those with a heart condition, traditional wood-burning saunas are the best, say Estonians, who deplore the predominance of modern Finnish electric saunas. For a start, there is ventilation, so the toxins you sweat out are carried away with the smoke from the logs; in a closed electric sauna, the toxins stay in the air, which is apparently why you feel fatigued after using one. Wood-burning saunas are, sadly, hard to find, and your best bet is to befriend someone lucky enough to have one at home, or perhaps in their country place. Most hotels have electrically powered saunas that non-residents can rent. One advantage is that they heat up quicker than the log type.

Reval Sport, Aia 20, **T** 641 2068, www.revalsport.ee.
Map 3, C5, p254

Status Club, Paldiski maantee 96, **T** 656 3911, www.statusclub.ee.
Map 1, E2, p250

Riding .

Tallinna Ratsaspordibaas, Paldiski maantee 135, **T** 656 3759. Children's lessons at weekends.

Niitra AS, Niitvälja, Harju County, **T** 671 6033.

Ruila Stable, Ruila village, Harju County, **T** 050 28473, www.hot.ee/ruilatall.

Raudoja Stable, Kuusalu, Harju County, **T** 607 2531.

Sailing

Pirita Marina, Regati puiestee 1, **T** 639 8980. *Map 1, B10, p251* The guarded visitor centre is well sheltered and has electricity, water, toilets, showers, a washing machine and a sauna.

Saunas

Beer House, Dunkri 5, **T** 627 6520, www.beerhouse.ee. *Sun-Thu 1100-2300, Fri and Sat 1100-0400. Map 2, H5, p253*

Club 26, Reval Hotel Olümpia, **T** 631 5585, www.revalhotels.com. *Mon-Fri 0630-2300, Sat and Sun 0730-2300. Map 3, J7, p255*

Kalma Saun, Vana-Kalamaja 9a, Liivalaia 33, **T** 627 1811, www.bma.ee/kalma. *1000-2300. Map 1, D5, p250*

Kempens, Raua 23, **T** 648 5436. *Wed-Sun 1100-2000. Map 1, E7, p250*

Skiing

Nõmme Ski Club, Vana-Mustamäe 16, **T** 670 0157. *Map 1, I3, p250*

Squash

City Squash, Tartu maantee 63, **T** 611 5510, www.citysquash.ee. *Mon-Fri 1200-2200, Sat and Sun 1000-2100. Map 1, E7, p251*

Surfing

Hawaii Express, **T** 623 7455, www.surf.ee. *Map 1, A10, p251* The best waves are about 20 km from Tallinn, in the bay at Vääna.

Swimming

Club 26, Reval Hotel Olümpia, Liivalaia 33, **T** 631 5585. *Mon-Fri 0630-2300, Sat and Sun 0730-2300. Map 3, J7, p255* Superb views from the 26th floor.

Kalev Spa and Water Park, Aia 18, **T** 649 3300, **F** 649 3301, www.kalevspa.ee. *90 EEK, children 70 EEK, under-6s free. Map 2, D/E9, p252* A high-tech, centrally located swimming and spa complex, with 50- and 25-m pools, three water slides, bubble baths with water massage, a children's pool with a mini slide, single-sex saunas (children also admitted), a gym and an endless menu of health and beauty treatments. Doors and lockers are operated electronically, with a bracelet you receive on arrival. Also a hotel on site, see p129.

Keila Health Centre, Paldiski maantee 17, Keila, **T** 673 7637, www.keilasport.ee. *0700-2200, Sat and Sun 0800-2200. Map 1, E5, p250*

Top Spa, Pirita Top Spa Hotel, **T** 639 8836, www.topspa.ee. *Mon-Fri 0630-2300, Sat and Sun 0800-2300. Map 1, B10, p251* Also sauna.

Tennis

Harjuoru Tennis Centre, Kaarli puiestee 2, **T** 645 2367. *Map 3, H2, p255*

Tallinn Tennis Hall, Regati puiestee 1, **T** 639 8814. *Map 1, B10, p251*

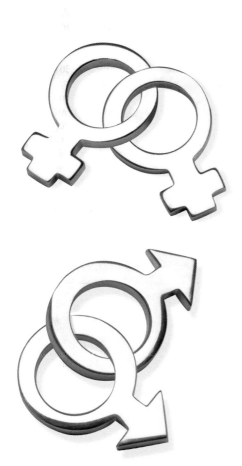

Although Tallinn is a tolerant city, it is some way behind Scandinavia and many northern European cities in terms of the atmosphere surrounding homosexuality. Many closet gays still do not feel confident enough to come out, partly because they fear, perhaps wrongly, that it might damage their career prospects. Older people remember the utter intolerance that was part of Soviet life. Gay Estonians who have spent time in countries that are more open about homosexuality are struck by the difference when they return home. That said, gay-bashing is rare (although some recommend discretion outside the protective walls of gay bars), and you are unlikely to come across people who make you feel awkward about being gay. It is almost as if it is not an issue. In summer, the main cruising spots are Harjumägi and Stroomi beach. Watch out for underage hustlers around the Balti jaam railway station, and be aware that AIDS, though not widespread, is on the increase, mainly as a result of intravenous drug use.

Associations

Estonian Association for Lesbians and Bisexual Women, **T** 055 11 132.

Estonian Gay League, **T** 653 4812.

GLIK (Gay and Lesbian Info Centre), Tartu Maantee 29, **T** 645 4545, www.gay.ee. *Mon-Fri 1400-2000, Sat 1200-1800, closed Sun*.

Bars and clubs

Angel, Sauna 1, **T** 641 6880, www.clubangel.ee. *Wed-Sat 2200-0500. Map 2, I7, p253*

G Punkt (G spot), Pärnu maantee 23. *Sun-Tue 1600-2400, Wed, Fri and Sat 1600-0200 Map 3, I3, p255* Pleasant lounge bar with Wednesday-night discos.

Nightman, Vineeri 4, www.nightman.ee (see also p171). *Map 1, F6, p250* Once known as a gay bar, now open to everyone.

Ring Club, Juhkentali 11, **T** 660 5490, www.ringclub.ee. *Map 3, K8, p255* Striptease, sauna and plenty of intimate nooks in this basement venue.

X-Baar, Sauna 1, **T** 620 9266, www.zone.ee/xbaar. *Open until at least 0100. Map 2, I6, p253* The city's longest-established gay bar is popular with Russian-speaking lesbians, Finnish sugar daddies and the odd male hustler. Fun, although it could do with better ventilation.

Gay and lesbian

Saunas

Club 69, Pärnu maantee 27, **T** 660 4830, www.gay.ee. *Sun-Thu 1600-0200, Fri, Sat 1600-0800.* *Map 3, I3, p255* Tallinn's first men-only sauna, and the first gay sauna-club in the Baltics, this is a friendly place much appreciated by foreigners. It has a café, a bar, a solarium and a TV lounge.

Websites

www.gay.ee General website for gay people in Estonia.

Estonians do not coo over children in public, but this is a child-friendly society that combines Scandinavian respect with quiet warmth and indulgence. Even the most formal restaurants are happy to cater for junior diners, while children are welcome in cafés and bars until 2100 (between 2300 and 0500 in summer and 0600 in winter nobody under 16 can enter without an adult), and nobody will frown at you for taking them to concerts so long as you leave if all hell breaks out.

The cobbled streets and narrow pavements of the Old Town make for bumpy buggy rides but, outside the historic centre, roads are even and pavements wider. Family taxis with children's seats are also available (just request in advance).

Larger department stores have children's playrooms and there are nappy-changing facilities at Stockmann (Liivalaia 53), Kaubamaja (Gonsiori 2), the Viru Keskus shopping centre, and the larger petrol stations. Tallinn is a green, relatively unpolluted city with parks and forests aplenty, an expanding network of cycle paths, and beaches within a 30-minute car or bus ride from the centre.

Nurseries/crèches

Finding an English-speaking babysitter is, well, child's play. Several nurseries have free places in summer, when local families are away (see below). Most of the larger hotels can also provide babysitting.

Ema ja Lapse Keskus (Centre for Mother and Child), Tuukri 11, **T** 528 3038, www.emalapsekeskus.ee. Supervised care for babies and children up to 8 years old.

Toome Eralasteaed, Toome puiestee 8, Nõmme, **T** 657 6082. *Daily 0730-1800.* A private nursery with a large garden in a leafy suburb 30 minutes from the city centre.

Vanalinna Lasteaed, Lai 9, **T** 641 2534. *Daily 0730-1800. Map 2, F5, p252* Old Town nursery for children aged 3 and up.

Sights

★ **City Wall and Defence Towers**, **T** 644 9867. *Jun-Aug Mon-Fri 1000-1900, Sat and Sun 1000-1700; May, Sep and Oct Mon-Fri 1200-1800, Sat and Sun 1100-1600; Mar, Apr and Nov Mon-Fri 1200-1700, Sat-Sun 1100-1600; Dec-Feb Mon-Fri 1200-1600, Sat and Sun 1100-1600. 7 EEK. Map 2, E4, p252* The short rampart walk to the Sauna and Kuldjala towers starts at the corner of Suur-Kloostri and Väike-Kloostri. See also p56.

Kadriorg Park. *Map 1, D8, p251* Rambling park with a lake where you can feed the swans.

★ **Rocca al Mare**, Vabaõhumuuseumi tee 12, **T** 654 9100. *May-Aug daily 1000-2000, buildings until 1800; Sep 1000-1800, buildings until 1700, Oct 1000-1800, buildings until 1600, Nov-Apr 1000-1700, buildings closed. 25 EEK in summer, 12 EEK in winter, free with Tallinn Card. Bus 21 from the centre. Map 1, E1, p250* Excellent open-air museum with folk-dancing, old farm buildings, bike hire and horse and cart rides. See also p87.

Tallinn Centre for Science and Technology, Põhja puiestee 29, **T** 715 2650, www.energiakeskus.ee. *Jun-Aug Mon-Fri 1000-1700; Sep-May Mon-Fri 1000-1700, Sat 1200-1700. 30 EEK, concessions and children 20 EEK, children 4-7 20 EEK, under-4s free; family ticket 80 EEK, free with Tallinn Card. Map 3, A4, p254* The emphasis here is on poking, prodding and splashing about, making it a sure-fire hit. The star attraction is the huge lightning conductor in the main hall; ask about demonstrations. See also pxx.

Tallinn City Museum, see Old Town, p54.

Tartu Mänguasjamuuseum, Lutsu 8, Tartu, **T** 746 1777, www.mm.ee. *Wed-Sun 1100-1800, playroom Wed-Sun 1100-1600.* Tartu's new Toy Museum, with a pretty wooden interior, is a lively place where children can paint, dress up or watch puppet films while parents take a nostalgic look at a well-illustrated history of toys.

Toy Museum, Kotzebue 16, Kalamaja **T** 641 3491. *Mar-Oct, Wed-Sun 1030-1800, Nov-Feb Wed-Sun 1030-1700. 10 EEK, concessions 5 EEK, under pre-school free; family ticket 20 EEK. Map 1, D5, p250* Children will especially enjoy the play area and Lego table.

TV Tower, see Pirita, p84.

Zoo, Paldiski maantee 145, Rocca al Mare, **T** 694 3300, www.tallinnzoo.ee. *May-Aug daily 0900-1900; Mar, Apr, Sep and Oct daily 0900-1700; Nov-Feb daily 0900-1500. 39 EEK, concessions 23 EEK, children 4 EEK, under-3s free; family ticket 82 EEK. Free with Tallinn Card. Map 1, F1, p250* Petting zoo, hamsters, rabbits and other furry creatures. See also p88.

Kids

Sleeping

Many hotels offer free beds for children up to a certain age. The most generous limit (up to 17 years) is at the **Radisson SAS**. The new **City Hotel Portus** has six family rooms and children under 16 stay free. There's a playroom in the lobby. The **Reval Hotel Central** has good rates and brightly furnished family rooms decorated with children's drawings. Children under 12 stay free when in their parents' room at several hotels, among them **Old Town Maestro's**, **Meriton Grand Hotel Tallinn**, **UniqueStay** and **Reval Olümpia**. **Poska Villa**, **Villa Stahl** and **Valge Villa** all have family-friendly suites or apartments. The **Must Kassi** camping site (see Sleeping, p137) has space for wee ones to run riot.

Arts and entertainment

Estonia National Opera, Estonia puiestee 4, **T** 626 0260, www.opera.ee. *Tickets 30-300 EEK; discounts Sat, Sun daytime and Tue, Wed evenings. Map 2, K8, p253* Programme includes children's musicals and Christmas shows.

Estonian National Puppet Theatre, Lai 1/3, **T** 667 9555, www.nukuteater.ee. *Tickets 35-75 EEK. Map 2, G4, p253* For children and teenagers: fairy tales, musicals and plays.

Kullo Children's Art Gallery, Kuninga 6, **T** 644 6873, www.kullo.ee. *Map 3, E/F3, p254* Hosts children's art exhibitions.

The **Linnateater** (see p184) and **Old Town Studio** (see p184) also offer children's shows.

Kids

Shopping

Nukupood, Raekoja plats 18, **T** 644 3058. *Mon-Sat 0900-1800, Sun 1100-1500. Map 2, H5, p253* This boutique sells wooden dolls' houses, dolls' house furniture, dolls and so on.

Sports and outdoor activities

Aura, Turu tänav 10, Tartu, **T** 730 0280. *Mon-Fri 0630-2200, Sat and Sun 0900-2200. 55-95 EEK children, family ticket 215-255 EEK.* State-of-the-art water park.

Haapsalu Veekeskus, Lihula maantee 10a, Haapsalu, www.spordibaasid.ee. *Mon-Fri 0630-2200, Sat and Sun 0800-2200. 30-60 EEK, family ticket 130-180 EEK.* Water slides, swimming pool.

Keila Health Centre, Paldiski maantee 17, Keila, **T** 673 7637, www.keilasport.ee. *Mon-Fri 0630-2200, Sat and Sun and holidays 0800-2200. 30-75 EEK. Map 1, E5, p250* Ultra-modern waterworld.

Nõmme Outdoor Centre, Jaama 12, Nõmme, **T** 677 0289, www.matkakeskus.ee. *Map 1, I3, p250* Canoe trips on the Valge and Jagala rivers, plus hiking and cross-country skiing.

Vembu-Tembu Land, Keskuse tee 2, Kurtna, Harjumaa, **T** 671 9155, www.vembu-tembumaa.ee. *Jun-Aug daily 1000-1900. Family ticket 175 EEK, free for under-3s.* Family amusement park 27 km from Tallinn.

Viimsi Tervis Health Spa (See p136). This hotel in Viimsi has a heated children's pool and a playroom for parents who want to swim or have beauty/health treatments.

Kids

Airline offices
Aeroflot (c/o Estonian Air) **T** 640 1160. **Air Baltic** (c/o Hermann Reisid travel agency), **T** 605 8887. **Air Livonia** (c/o Estair), **T** 640 1160. **American Airlines** (c/o Finnair), **T** 605 8353. **British Airways** (c/o Finnair), **T** 605 8353. **Czech Airlines** (CSA), **T** 630 9397. **Estair**, **T** 605 8887. **Estonian Air**, **T** 640 1160. **Finnair**, **T** 605 8353. **Lithuanian Airlines**, www.lal.lt. **Lot Polish Airlines**, **T** 681 4561. **SAS**, **T** 605 8887.

Banks and ATMs
There's no shortage of banks (*pank* in Estonian) and ATMs in Tallinn. Most banks are open 0900-1700/1800 weekdays and some on Saturday, 1000-1500. Cash machines are available at most banks. There are handy ATMs on Vabaduse väljak, Raekoja plats and Pikk street, but you will find them all over town.

The main banks are situated on Vabaduse väljak and Liivalaia. All offer currency exchange. There are also money-changing offices in the larger supermarkets and hotels, and at the railway station, the harbour and the airport. American Express, Eurocheque and Thomas Cook traveller's cheques are generally accepted (although not in shops). Most hotels, shops and restaurants take credit cards (American Express, Diner's Club, Eurocard, Mastercard and Visa).

Bicycle hire
Adventuur, Kunderi 8a, **T** 527 0966, www.adventuur.ee (for cycling trips). **City Bike Tours**, Tallinn City Camping, Pirita tee, **T** 051 11819, www.citybike.ee. *May-Sep.* **Dreisi**, Tartu maantee 73, **T** 637 6779. **Hawaii Express**, Regati puiestee 1, Pirita, **T** 639 8508, www.hawaii.ee. **Matkaexpert**, Mustamäe tee 60, **T** 656 3760, www.matkaexpert.ee. **Nõmme Matkakeskus**, Jaama 12, **T** 051 52336, www.matkakeskus.ee (also rental of skis, tents and camping equipment).

Car hire

The following all have offices at the airport (offices in town are listed in brackets): **Avis**, **T** 667 1515, www.avis.ee (Liivalaia 13/15, **T** 667 1500); **Budget** , **T** 605 8600, www.budget.ee; **Europcar**, **T** 605 8031; **Evison**, **T** 605 8059, www.evison.ee; **Hertz**, **T** 605 8923, www.hertz.ee; **National**, **T** 605 8071, www.nationalcar.ee. Local firms include **Sir Autorent**, Juhkentali 11, **T** 661 4353, www.sirrent.ee; and **Tulikarent**, Tihase 34, **T** 612 0012, www.tulikatakso.ee.

Credit card lines

If you lose a card, **Card Centre of Banks** (Pankade Kaardiskeskuse) can help with informing banks abroad, in addition to other credit card-related problems, **T** 671 1477, www.estcard.ee.

Cultural institutions

British Council, Vana-Posti 7, **T** 625 7788, www.britishcouncil.ee. *Tue-Sat 1200-1745*. **Danish Cultural Institute**, Vene 14, **T** 646 6373. *Mon-Fri 1000-1600. Danish film evenings third Tue of the month*. **Estonian Institute**, **T** Suur-Karja 14, **T** 631 4355, www.einst.ee. *Mon-Fri 1000-1700*. **Finnish Institute**, Harju 1, **T** 631 3917, www.finst.ee. *Mon-Fri 1000-1600*. **French Cultural Centre**, Kuninga 4, **T** 627 1190, www.france.ee. *Mon-Thu 1200-1900, Fri 1200-1800*. **Goethe-Institute Tallinn**, Suurtüki 4b, **T** 627 6960, www.goethe.de/tallinn. *Mon-Thu 0900-1300, 1400-1700, Fri 0900-1300*.

Dentists

Baltic Medical Partners, Tartu maantee 32, **T** 601 0550, www.bmp.ee. *Mon-Fri 0830-1900*. **CityMed Hambakliinik**, Ahtri 8, **T** 661 6333, www.citymed.ee. *Mon-Thu 0800-2000, Fri 0800-1700*. **Kentmanni Hambaravi**, Kentmanni 11a, **T** 644 0186. *Mon-Fri 0800-1800, weekend emergency appointments*. **Tallinna Hambapolikliinik**, Toompuiestee 4, **T** 611 9230.

Mon-Fri 0800-2000, Sat and Sun 0900-1800. **Vanalinna Hambaravi**, Pikk 7, **T** 644 3010, *Mon-Fri 0900-1800*.

Disabled
Tallinn is making progress in catering for the disabled: most of the larger hotels have suitable rooms and facilities. The Old Town, however, is difficult to negotiate in a wheelchair. For more specific information, contact the local society for the disabled, **Tallinn City's Board of Disabled People** (Tallinna Puuetega Inimeste koda), Endla 59, **T** 655 4161, www.tallinnakoda.ee.

Doctors
Contact the hospital (see below) or **Sinu-Arst-Family Doctor Practice**, Narva maantee 7, 3rd floor, **T** 631 5440. EU citizens should bring their European Health Insurance Cards.

Electricity
Estonia functions on the continental 220V mains supply.

Embassies
Australia, Marja 9, **T** 650 9308. **Canada**, Toom-Kooli 13, **T** 627 3311. **Finland**, Kohtu 4, **T** 610 3200. **Ireland**, Vene 2, **T** 681 1888. **Latvia**, Tõnismägi 10, **T** 627 7850. **Lithuania**, Uus 15, **T** 631 4030. **Russia**, Pikk 19, **T** 646 4175. **Sweden**, Pikk 28, **T** 640 5600. **UK**, Wismari 6, **T** 667 4700. **USA**, Kentmanni 20, **T** 668 8100.

Emergency numbers
Police, **T** 110. Fire and ambulance, **T** 112. Coastguard, **T** 692 2222.

Hospitals
East-Tallinn Central Hospital (Ida-Tallinna Keskhaigla), Ravi 18, **T** 620 7015. **Tallinn Children's Hospital**, Tervise 28, **T** 697 7146 (reception), **T** 697 7194 (trauma-point registration),

T 697 7113 (information). **First Aid information hotline**, T 697 1145 (24 hrs).

Information line
T 118. Useful for general enquiries.

Internet/email
Internet access is available at most hotels and at the **Kaubamaja** and **Stockmann** department stores (see shopping); the **Central Post Office**; the **National Library of Estonia**, ground floor, Tõnismägi 2, T 630 7381, *Mon, Thu 1000-1700, Tue, Wed, Fri 1200-1900;* **Coffe IN** Suur-Karju 13, T 53 3315 75. 15 minutes 15 EEK, 1 hour 30 EEK, and at **Tallinn airport**. Many cafés and hotels have WiFi spots; for details, visit www.wifi.ee.

Language schools
Language Centre Tea, Liivalaia 28, T 645 9207, www.tea.ee. **Tallinn Language School**, Endla 22, T 662 0706, www.tallinnakeeltekool.ee. **Tartu University**, Ülikooli 18, www.ut.ee/av/summer.

Left luggage
Old City Harbour, Sadama 25, T 631 8550, has 24-hour lockers and a luggage room in A and D terminals, *daily 0800-2100*. There are also left-luggage facilities in the basement of **Tallinn Bus Station** (Tallinna Autobussijaam), Lastekodu 46 (trams 2 or 4), T 681 3471, *daily 0630-2230*; and at **Stockmann** department store, fifth floor.

Libraries
National Library of Estonia, Tõnismägi 2, T 630 7611, *Mon-Fri 1000-2000, Sat 1200-1900. Jul-Aug Mon-Fri 1200-1900 (day pass 5 EEK)*. **Tallinn Central Library**, T 683 0900, Estonia puiestee 8, *Mon-Fri 1000-1900, Sat 1000-1700 (day pass 5 EEK)*.

Lost property

There is no lost-property office. Best try the police (see below).

Media

The European editions of English-language newspapers are available on the day at kiosks and larger hotels. National editions arrive a day or two late, except the *Financial Times*, which is printed in Stockholm and usually available by the afternoon. Estonian television has three Estonian-language terrestrial channels. ETV is the equivalent of the BBC. Most hotels have satellite TV, BBC World and CNN.

The bimonthly *In Your Pocket* guide, available at the tourist office, has good accommodation, restaurant and bar listings. The bimonthly *City Paper*, www.balticsww.com, has listings and news for Tallinn, Riga and Vilnius. *The Baltic Times* is a weekly newspaper. *Tallinn This Week*, www.ttw.ee, is a free brochure with tourist information and basic listings. *Life in Estonia*, www.esto.info, is a magazine that aims to familiarize visitors with the local economy and culture. *Global Estonian*, quarterly, contains features on Estonian culture and politics for Estonians abroad, www.eestimaja.ee/ge.

Pharmacies (late-night)

Tõnismäge Apteek, Tõnismägi 5, **T** 644 2282, *Mon-Sat 0900-2000*, has a 24-hour emergency service. **Aia Apteek**, Aia 10, **T** 627 3607, *Mon-Fri 0800-2400, Sat 0830-2400, Sun 0900-2400*. **Revali Raeapteek**, Raekoja plats 11, **T** 631 4860, *Mon-Fri 0900-1900, Sat 0900-1700*. There's a pharmacy in the **Melon** shopping centre, Estonia puiestee 1, **T** 630 6699, *Mon-Fri 0900-2000, Sat 1000-2000, Sun 1000-1800*. In Estonia, you need a prescription for anti-histamine cream, so bring some with you.

Police

The **Police Prefecture of Tallinn** (headquarters) is at Pärnu maantee 139, **T** 612 4444. Police emergency is **T** 110. **Tallinn Central Police Station** is at Pärnu maantee 11, **T** 612 4205.

Post offices

The city's main post office is the large grey building on the north side of Viru väljak, Narva Maantee 1, *Mon-Fri 0730-2000, Sat 0900-1800, Sun 0900-1500*. There is also a post office on Lossi plats, Toompea, *Mon-Fri 0900-1700*. A first-class stamp for Europe costs 6.50 EEK, or 6 EEK for a postcard; for North America, it's 8 EEK/7.50 EEK. Visit www.post.ee for further details.

Public holidays

1 January, New Year's Day; 24 February, Independence Day; Good Friday; Easter Sunday; 1 May, Spring Day; Whitsunday; 23 June, Victory Day (commemorates battle of Võnnu, 1919, when Estonian forces foiled an attempt to restore Baltic German control over the region); 24 June, St John's Day; 20 August, Restoration of Independence Day; 25 December, Christmas Day; 26 December.

Religious services

Most churches post the times outside. In English, Sundays 1500 at Pühavaimu. See also individual churches in Sights.

Student organizations

Federation of Estonian Student Unions, Gonsiori 9, **T** 660 1688, www.eyl.ee. *Mon-Fri 0900-1700*. **AIESEC** (International Association for Students of Economy and Business), Akadeemia tee 7-104, **T** 620 3625, www.aiesec.ee. **BEST Estonia** (Board of European Students of Technology), Ehitajate tee 5, 19086 Tallinn, **T** 620 3625, www.best.ee. **Erasmus Student Network Tartu**, c/o Tartu University Student Council, Ülikooli 18a, Tartu 50090, **T** 534 20630, www.esn.ee/tartu. **Student Union** (Tartu University), Ülikooli 18b, Tartu 50090, **T** 737 5400, www.ut.ee/esindus.

Telephone

All landline numbers in Estonia are now seven digits and are shown as such in this guide. When calling from abroad, the international prefix for Estonia is +372. So from the UK, you would need to dial the UK access code (00), followed by the Estonia code (+372), followed by the number. Public telephones only take cards, available from kiosks, hotels and the post office (50 EEK and 100 EEK). For directory enquiries and cinema schedules, dial **T** 1188, **T** 1184, **T** 1182 or the only free enquiry number, **T** 626 1111. For mobile phones, pick up a starter kit with a prepaid local card, such as *Simpel*, from a telephone shop (also at the airport). Calls to local mobiles from land lines can be very expensive.

Time
Estonia uses Eastern European Time, two hours ahead of GMT all year round.

Tipping
Not obligatory, but 10-15% is most welcome in restaurants (tip in cash if you want the money to go to the right person), and it is common to round up taxi fares.

Toilets
There are public toilets in Toompea (in the small park near Pikk Hermann, next to the Riigikogu building); at the entrance to the Troika restaurant, on Raekoja plats (disabled), in the Viru Keskus shopping centre, and on Valli street (near Viru), as well as in the Stockmann and Kaubamaja department stores (see Shopping) and at the railway station.

Tour operators
Estonian Holidays, Parnu maantee 12, **T** 631 4109, www.holidays.ee. **Estravel/American Express Centre**, Suur-Karja 15, **T** 626 6266, www.estravel.ee. Fixed and tailor-made tours, including a survival week on a farm and a helicopter tour to islands of your choice. **ETFL** (Estonian Association of Travel Agencies), **T** 631 3013, www.etfl.ee. **Fix**

Indeed, Pärnu maantee 67a, **T** 681 9977, www.fixindeed.ee, offers day tours to southern and eastern Estonia, including trips to ostrich farms. **Lahemaa** Historian, nature and folklore expert Anne Kurepalu (**T** 323 4100/569 13786, anne@phpalmse.ee) offers lively tours with car for 500-900 EEK per day. She also takes tourists to other parts of Estonia's north coast and to Tartu, Lake Peipsi and Tallinn. **Maremark**, L Koidula 38, **T** 601 3446, contact@maremark.ee, www.maremark.ee. Diving courses, trips, events and equipment. There are 40,000 sunken ships in Estonian waters, many preserved through low concentration of oxygen in the water, plus rocks, craters, eels and crayfish. **Tartu Baltic Tours**, Pikk 31, Tartu, **T** 630 0400, www.bt.ee.

Transport enquiries

Airport, **T** 605 8888 (flight information), www.tallinn-airport.ee. **Tallinn Bus Station**, **T** 680 0900, www.bussireisid.ee. **Eurolines coaches T** 680 0909, www.eurolines.ee. **Railway station**, **T** 1447, international tickets **T** 615 6850. **Linnahall** (hydrofoils to Helsinki): **T** 699 9333, www.lindaliini.ee. **Old City Harbour T** 631 8454, www.portoftallinn.ee. For details of buses in and around Tallinn, call **T** 1345 or visit www.tak.ee. For trains around Tallinn and in Harju county, contact **Electric Railway** (Elektriraudtee), **T** 1447, www.elektriraudtee.ee. For trams and trolley buses, contact **Tallinn Tram and Trolleybus Company Ltd**, **T** 697 6222 (trolleybuses), **T** 697 6333 (trams), www.ttk.ee.

Travel agents

Baltic Holidays, 40 Princes Street, Manchester, M1 6DE, **T** 0870 7579233, www.balticholidays.com.
Cox & Kings, **T** 020 7873 5000, www.coxandkings.co.uk.
Explore Worldwide, 1 Frederik St, Aldershot, Hants GU11 1LQ, **T** 01252 760100, www.exploreworldwide.com.
Fregata Holidays, **T** 020 7420 7305, www.fregatatravel.co.uk.
Great Escapes, **T** 0845 330 2057, www.greatescapes.co.uk.

Kirker, **T** 020 7231 3333, www.kirkerholidays.com.
Limosa Holidays, **T** 01263 578143, www.limosaholidays.co.uk.
Martin Randall, 10 Barley Mow Passage, Chiswick, London W4
4PH, **T** 020 8724 3355, www.martinrandall.co.uk.
Naturetrek, **T** 01962 733051, www.naturetrek.co.uk.
On the Go Tours, **T** 020 7371 1113, www.onthegotours.com.
Original Travel, **T** 020 7978 7333, www.originaltravel.co.uk.
Regent Holidays, 15 John Street, Bristol BS1 2HR, **T** 0117 921
1711, **F** 0117 925 4866, www.regent-holidays.co.uk.
Scantours UK, Clareville House, 47 Whitcomb Street, London
WC2H 7DH, **T** 020 7839 2927, **F** 020 7839 5891,
www.scantours.co.uk.
Specialised Tours, 4 Copthorne Bank, Copthorne, Crawley, West
Sussex RH10 3QX, **T** 01342 712785, www.specialisedtours.com.
Thomson City Breaks, **T** 0870 888 0225, www.thomsoncities.co.uk.
Travel for the Arts, **T** 020 8799 8350, www.travelforthearts.co.uk.

A sprint through history

8000 BC	The ancestors of the Estonian people arrive in the area; the oldest evidence of a settlement on the site of present-day Tallinn dates back to c3500 BC.
1st century AD	Roman historian Tacitus refers to the "Aestii" people and the "unfamiliar" language they speak.
AD 100-400	Trade links established with Poland, Finland, Latvia, Lithuania and Russia. A port is established on the Pirita River in the 2nd century.
7th century	Creation of Iru fortress near present-day Lasnamäe.
AD 800-1200	Trade develops with northwest Europe and, via Russia, the Orient. A fortress is built on Toompea in the 11th century.
1154	Arab traveller al-Idrisi marks "Koluvan" (Tallinn) on his map of the world.
1199	The Pope calls for a crusade against pagans in the Baltic area: Danes, Germans, Russians and Swedes vie for domination.
1208-27	Estonians fight against German, Swedish, Danish and Russian invaders, but are overwhelmed and converted to Christianity. In 1219, King Waldemar II of Denmark takes Tallinn after a fierce battle against Estonians in the north. According to legend, the Danes were on the back foot until a red banner with a white cross descended from the sky, rallying them enough for victory and inspiring the Danish flag.
1238	Danish rule is established in northern Estonia. The Livonian Order and assorted clerical states control central and southern Estonia.

1242	The forces of Russian prince Alexander Nevsky defeat the Livonian Order on the frozen wastes of Lake Peipsi, putting an end to their eastward expansion.
13th-14th centuries	Tallinn and other Estonian cities, including Tartu, Pärnu and Haapsalu, join the Hanseatic League.
1346	After the St George's Night uprising (1343), the Danes sell their territory in Estonia to the Teutonic Order. It then passes to the Livonian Order, which rules it until 1561.
1558-82	The Livonian War: Denmark, Poland, Russia and Sweden battle for Estonia. Sweden wins, heralding the progressive "good old Swedish days". The first grammar school is opened in Tallinn in 1631; Tartu University is founded in 1632.
1700	Start of the Great Northern War: Peter the Great craves access to the Baltic; Sweden battles Russia, Denmark, Poland and Saxony. Despite an early victory in Narva in 1700, the Swedes fail to hold their territory in Estonia; Tartu is razed in 1708.
1710	Russian troops seize Tallinn. Two centuries of Tsarist rule begin.
1739	The Bible is printed in Estonian.
1816	Tsar Alexander I abolishes serfdom, giving Estonian peasants the chance to own farms.
1857	The first Estonian-language newspaper, *Perno Postimees* ('Pärnu Herald'), is published.
1862	Inspired by Finland's *Kalevala* and a wealth of local legends, Estonian intellectuals led by Faehlmann

(1798-1850) and Kreutzwald (1803-82) create a national epic, *Kalevipoeg* (Son of Kalev).

1869   The first Song Festival, an expression of the growing National Awakening, takes place in Tartu.

1870   The Tallinn-St Petersburg railway is finished, marking the beginning of Estonian industrialization.

1881-94   The accession of Tsar Alexander III leads to a period of intense Russification. In 1882, Russia becomes the official language in all Estonian institutions. In 1894, work begins on the historicist Alexander Nevsky Cathedral, on Toompea.

1905   First Russian Revolution: the Tsar's army brutally suppresses a peaceful demonstration near the present-day Estonia Theatre.

1917   Amid chaos in Russia after the October Revolution, the Estonian National Congress proclaims its superiority over Russian authorities.

1918   Estonia declares its independence on 24 February, after the Russian retreat. German troops occupy Estonia until the collapse of the German Empire in November. On 16 November, the Red Army launches an attack on Estonia, beginning the 13-month Independence War: with help from Britain and Finland, Estonia fends off both German and Red Russian invaders. The provisional government holds elections in spring 1919.

1920	Soviet Russia signs the Tartu Peace Treaty and forever renounces claims on Estonia. The Republic of Estonia approves its constitution in June.
Mid 1930s	Communist and fascist sympathizers are active in Estonia. A series of political crises results in increasingly authoritarian presidential rule.
1939	On 23 August, Germany and the Soviet Union sign the Molotov-Ribbentrop Pact. Secret protocols pave the way for Russia's annexation of the Baltic countries, in breach of the Tartu Peace Treaty. Russia swiftly establishes military bases in Estonia. On 14 June 1940, the USSR forcibly annexes Estonia. In 1941, 9,600 Estonians are deported to Siberia.
1941	On 22 August, Germany occupies Estonia.
1944	Soviet planes bomb Tallinn on 9 March. By September, German forces retreat. The Estonian Republic is redeclared on 18 September, but Soviet forces reoccupy Estonia on 22 September. An estimated 75,000 Estonians flee to Germany or Sweden, fearing the return of Soviet rule; another 36,000 are arrested and accused of aiding the Nazis. Up to 35,000 Forest Brothers resist the occupation from bases in the forests; the last one dies in 1978.
1949	A further 20,702 Estonians are deported to Siberia in an effort to quash resistance to the collectivization of farms and to the Stalinist regime.
1979	Protesters submit a proposal to restore the Baltic countries' independence to the UN, USSR and NATO.

1980	Moscow Olympic Games: Pirita is chosen as the site for the Olympic regatta and the Olümpia Hotel and airport are built as a showcase for foreign guests.
1987	On 23 August, protesters declare that Estonia is occupied and call for the restoration of independence. The details of the Molotov-Ribbentrop pact are exposed for the first time.
1988	The Singing Revolution gathers pace, with night-time demonstrations in the Song Festival Grounds, one of which unites 300,000 demonstrators.
1989	The Estonian flag flies from Pikk Hermann on 24 February, Independence Day. On 23 August, two million people form a human chain from Tallinn to Vilnius, the Lithuanian capital, to mark the 50th anniversary of the Molotov-Ribbentrop pact.
1991	On 20 August, the day after the hardline coup in Moscow, Estonia declares independence. On 6 September, Russia follows the rest of the world and recognizes Estonia's independence. On 17 September, Estonia joins the UN.
1992	Estonia adopts a democratic constitution. Parliamentary and presidential elections are held. The country introduces its own currency, the kroon.
1995	Free Trade Agreement with the EU comes into effect.
2001	Estonia wins the Eurovision Song Contest.
2004	Estonia joins EU a few weeks after becoming a member of Nato.

Books

During the Soviet era, Estonia had one of the most liberal literary climates in the Soviet Union. Solzhenitsyn wrote much of *The Gulag Archipelago* in hiding in southern Estonia (it was eventually published in Paris), while Bulgakov's magnum opus, *The Master and Margherita*, was first published in Tallinn (1969).

Estonian literature's gradual release from having to be political (resisting totalitarianism via innuendo and allegory) began in the 1980s. The dreary pointlessness of daily life during the period of stagnation (1968-87) was the inspiration for Peeter Sauter's book *Indigo* (1990). In the early 1990s, authors focused on Soviet crimes, such as deportation and life in camps and prisons, before moving on to the physically intimate side of romantic relations, something untouched in occupation-era literature. Former deportee Jaan Kross, who, along with poet Jaan Kaplinski, has been put forward for the Nobel Prize, is the most internationally acclaimed contemporary Estonian author. Reorientation to the west and the freedom to travel has led to new literary influences and more experimental works; Jüri Ehlvest and Toomas Raudam, for example, explore the aesthetics and structure of the novel. There is also a tradition for magic realism and absurdist writing: the world looks strange, even grotesque, through the eyes of writers such as Arvo Valton and Mehis Heinsaar. Several Russian-language writers also work in Tallinn.

Poetry has always been hugely important in Estonia. In the 1970s and 1980s, Hando Runnel gave voice to national resistance; contemporary poets of note include Doris Kareva and Jaan Kaplinski, the only Estonian poet whose collections are readily available in English. His free-form work, which shows the influence of both western modernism and classic Chinese poetry, combines closely observed nature with spiritual and political reflection.

Sadly, although many Estonian works have been translated into Swedish, German and French, there is a sorry shortage of books in English translation. Perhaps the only two names known in the

English-speaking world are Kross and Kaplinski. Viivi Luik's acclaimed *The Beauty of History* (1991), about the events of 1968, has still to find a publisher, despite having been translated into English. To see what you're missing, get hold of the English-language *Estonian Literary Magazine*, which publishes extracts from contemporary works; for a free subscription, contact the **Estonian Institute**, **T** 631 4355, www.einst.ee. Information in English about Estonian writing is also available at the **Estonian Literature Information Centre**, **T** 631 4870, www.estlit.ee.

Anthologies

Estonian Short Stories: Writings from an Unbound Europe, ed Pruul, K and Reddaway, D (1996), Northwestern University Press, Illinois. Includes stories by Kross, Valton, Mati Unt, Raudam and Ehlvest.

From Baltic Shores (1994), ed Christopher Moseley, Norvik Press, Surrey, England. Short stories by Unt, Valton and others.

Les Hirondelles: anthologie des nouvelles estoniennes contemporaines (2002), Presses Universitaires de Caen. In French. Short stories by 19 Estonian writers, including Andrus Kivirähk, Mehis Heinsaar and Mati Unt.

The Sailors' Guardian (1984), Perioodika, Tallinn. Short stories from the Soviet era.

Biography and travelogues

Hillier, P, *Arvo Pärt* (1997), Oxford University Press. Definitive biography of Estonia's most famous contemporary composer, written by a pioneering conductor who has worked closely with him.

Ross, A, *The Winter Sea* (1997), Harvill. Memoir-cum-travelogue by the late editor of the *London Magazine*, with poetry and chapters on Tallinn and Haapsalu.

Rumessen, V, *Eduard Tubin ja tema aeg* (2005), SE&JS. Illustrated biography of the composer Eduard Tubin (1905-82), with plenty of information about his time and sections in English.

Contemporary fiction translated into English

Dolvlatov, S, *Compromise* (1983), Knopf. Savagely comic account of a talented, if dissolute, journalist ground down by the censors in 1970s Tallinn. The Bashkiria-born author's association with Estonian dissidents forced him to emigrate to America.

Kross, J, *The Czar's Madman* (1992), Harvill. Superb critique of Soviet rule via the story of a Baltic German aristocrat who dares to criticize the Tsar. A modern classic.
    The Conspiracy and Other Stories (1995), Harvill. Painful, wryly humorous tales about the tragic experience of Estonians under Soviet and Nazi occupation.
    Professor Martin's Departure (1994), HarperCollins. The injustices of late-19th-century Russia.
    Treading Air (2003), Harvill. The narrative unfolds in stories related by 70-year-old Ullo Paerand, who relates the violence and political upheaval of the Soviet and Nazi occupations, explaining how a wall of silence came to be built between western and eastern Europe.

Õnnepalu, T, *Border State* (2000), Northwestern University Press, Illinois. A young gay Estonian translator's adventures in Paris. Elegantly written, with pithy observations on the difference between consumer-oriented westerners and prickly easterners.

Palmer, W, *The Good Republic* (1990), Secker & Warburg. Set in an imaginary Baltic capital, this is a painfully convincing account of the horrors of Soviet and Nazi occupation, and the compromises that accompanied them.

Unt, M, *The Autumn Ball* (1985), Perioodika, Tallinn. First Estonian postmodernist novel, about the musings of six very different characters living in the tower blocks of Mustamäe. A fragmentary work that captures the atmosphere of a Soviet-built estate. The English translation was published after Uut's sudden death in 2005.

History

Captain Agar, A, *Baltic Episode* (1963), Hodder and Stoughton. A British secret agent's dramatic account of how the Royal Navy helped secure Estonia's independence in the face of threats from Russia and Germany in 1919.

Lieven, A, *The Baltic Revolution* (1993), Yale University Press. Classic (and weighty) tome about the return to independence by *The Times*'s man in the Baltics.

Seth, R, *Baltic Corner: Travels in Estonia* (1938), Methuen. Priceless observations from an English gentleman.

Thomson, C, *The Singing Revolution* (1991), Michael Joseph. Personal, eye-witness account of the restoration of independence in the Baltic states.

Language

Ahi, H, and **Pesti**, M, *E nagu Eesti (E like Estonia), Estonian for Beginners*, TEA Publishers, Tallinn. Local publication with a cassette and a separate book for teachers.

Moseley, C, *Colloquial Estonian: A Complete Language Course* (1994), Routledge. Clear, practical book, suitable for self-study or classwork.

Oinas, FJ, *Basic Course in Estonian* (1975), Bloomington: Indiana University Press. User-friendly classic, packed with exercises.

Oser, W, and **Salasoo**, T, *Estonian for Beginners* (1987), Council of Estonian Societies in Australia. For class or individual study. Cassettes available.

Poetry

Kaplinski, J, *The Same Sea in us All* (1990), Harvill; *The Wandering Border* (1992), Harvill; *Through the Forest* (1996), Harvill; *Windship with Oars of Light* (2001), Huma, Tallinn. *Evening Brings Everything Back* (2004), Highgreen: Bloodaxe Books; *I Am the Spring in Tartu* (1991), Laurel Press.

Language

Estonian, once voted one of the most beautiful languages in the world (although nobody quite seems to remember when), belongs to the Baltic-Finnic group of the Finno-Ugrian family of languages, which includes Finnish, Hungarian and Lapp. It is spoken by about one million people in Estonia and 100,000 *väliseestlased*, or Estonians living abroad, mainly in Sweden, North America, Australia and Germany, but also in the UK.

Estonians won't be at all surprised or upset if you can't speak their language, but every effort will be greeted with enthusiasm (well, as much enthusiasm as your average reserved Estonian can muster at a first meeting). About 40% of Tallinn's population is said to be Russian-speaking, though, increasingly, younger Russians speak Estonian as well as English, which is by far the most popular foreign language. One prevailing myth is that Estonians will bite your head off for speaking Russian: ask politely if you can, and most of those who know Russian will do so if it means being able to communicate. Russian, as well as Estonian, is spoken at Tallinn's train and bus stations.

The letters C, F, X, Y and Z do not exist in Estonian. If you're looking something up in a telephone directory, be warned that words beginning with the following accented letters come after W (the last non-accented word in the Estonian alphabet), in this order: õ, ä, ö, ü. The letter 'õ', a sound that comes from a nether region deep in the throat, is near impossible for English-speakers to emulate. Think of *ir* in the word 'bird' and you're almost there.

The first syllable in a word is almost always accented (exceptions include foreign and loan words), which gives the language its distinctive bouncy, rhythmical sound.

Pronunciation
Estonian is pronounced pretty much as it looks, although 'j' is usually 'y' (eg 'ja', or yes, is pronounced 'yah').
Accented vowels can be tricky:
õ like 'ir' in 'bird'; ä like 'a' in 'cat'; ö like 'er' in 'ermine'; ü like 'oo' in 'boot'.

Basic words and phrases
Hello *Tere*
Good morning *Tere hommikust*
Goodnight *Head ööd* (Hey-add erd)
Goodbye *Head aega* (literally, good time) or *nägemist* (see you)
Yes *Ja* (yah)
No *Ei* (like saying the letter 'a')
Thank you *Tänan*, or the less formal and widely used *aitäh* (I-tah)
Please *Palun*
Excuse me/sorry *Vabandust*

Do you speak English? *Kas teie räägite inglise keelt?*
Does anyone here speak English? *Kas keegi räägib inglise keelt?*
I don't know *Ma ei tea*
Where is … ? *Kus on … ?*
Can you help me? *Palun kas te saate mind aidata?*
How much does… cost? *Kui palju … maksab?*
When does … open/close? *Mis kell … avatakse/suletakse?*
I would like … *Ma tahaksin …*
One ticket, please *Üks pilet, palun*
Two tickets, please *Kaks piletit, palun*

Emergencies
Help! *Aidake! Appi!*
Where is the police station? *Kus on politsei?*
I'm unwell *Ma olen haige*
I need a doctor *Mul on vaja arsti*

Getting around/recognizing signs

Tänav Street	*Puiestee* Avenue
Maantee Boulevard	*Väljak* Square
Kesklinn Town centre	*Takso* Taxi
Trollibuss Trolleybus	*Tramm* Tram
Buss Bus	*Lähtekoht* Departure
Sihtkoht Destination	*Apteek* Chemist
Pood/kauplus Shop	*Avatud/Suletud* Open/closed
N (*Naised*) Female toilets	M (*Mehed*) Male toilets

Days of the week

Monday *Esmaspäev*	Tuesday *Teisipäev*
Wednesday *Kolmapäev*	Thursday *Neljapäev*
Friday *Reede*	Saturday *Laupäev*
Sunday *Pühapäev*	

Eating out

You shouldn't have any trouble ordering in English in Tallinn, Tartu, Pärnu or Haapsalu, and many restaurants (not just the tourist traps) have menus in English. In more remote rural areas, menus are likely to be in Estonian only.

I don't eat meat *Ma ei söö liha*
What do you want to drink? *Mida soovite juua?*
A beer, please *Üks õlu, palun*
A glass of white/red wine *Üks klaas valget/punast veini*
Cheers *Tervist*
The bill, please *Arve, palun*

The menu

Eelroad Starters	*Magustoidud* Desserts
Suupisted Snacks	*Taimetoidud* Vegetarian

Estonian specialities

Sült Meat jelly (usually veal)
Hapukapsas Sauerkraut
Heeringas hapukoorega Herring with sour cream
Suitsukala Smoked fish
Kalamari Fish roe

Meat *Liha*

Kalkun Turkey	*Kana* Chicken
Sealiha Pork	*Veiseliha* Beef
Biifsteak Steak	*Sink* Ham
Pardiliha Duck	*Lambaliha* Lamb/mutton

Fish *Kala*

Ahven Perch	*Forell* Trout
Koha Pike-perch	*Lestafilee* Plaice fillet
Lõhe Salmon	

Fruit and vegetables

Kukeseened Chanterelles
Õun Apple
Maasikas Strawberry
Porgand Carrot
Salat Salad
Sibul Onion

Puravik Ceps
Apelsin Orange
Kurk Cucumber
Kartul Potato
Seened Mushrooms
Küüslauk Garlic

Drinks

Tee Tea
Piim Milk
Siider Cider
Punane vein Red wine
*Mineraalvesi gaasiga/
gaasita* Sparkling/
still mineral water

Kohv Coffee
Õlu Beer
Valge vein White wine
Õunamahl Apple juice

Other

Kook Cake
Võileib Sandwich
Jäätis Ice cream
Sai White bread
Juust Cheese
Riis Rice

Leib Bread
Suhkur Sugar
Leib Rye bread
Supp Soup
Pannkoogid Pancakes

Numbers

One *Üks*
Two *Kaks*
Three *Kolm*
Four *Neli*
Five *Viis*

Six *Kuus*
Seven *Seitse*
Eight *Kaheksa*
Nine *Üheksa*
Ten *Kümme*

Enjoy the silence

It may not have been written with Estonians in mind, but Depeche Mode's chart-topping single 'Enjoy the Silence' could almost be the country's national anthem: its chorus, "Words are very / Unnecessary / They can only do harm", has the feel of an ancient Estonian proverb. No wonder there's a bar in Tallinn that bears the band's name (and, until recently, played only Depeche Mode songs).

Estonians love silence and, like Greta Garbo, they want to be alone. When the javelin thrower Andrus Värnik won Estonia's first World Championship gold medal in 2005, his coach was asked how he felt about this unprecedented success. He replied: "I thought how nice it is to sit, to be alone, and to think about how good it is." Estonians can sit in company without talking for minutes on end and later remember the occasion as a delightful, even exciting, one. An Italian visitor to Estonia once complained of his time there: "Nobody talks!" Not talking has advantages, especially for Estonian men, who live in horror of saying the wrong thing or making fools of themselves. It eliminates the need for small talk, too. When Estonians do speak, they are direct. Ask someone how they are and don't be surprised to hear: "Not at all well." (This sometimes scares Americans.) Estonians are adept at dead-pan irony and a twinkle in the eye should tell you that a joke is being made, quite possibly at your expense. If you can laugh at yourself, you will charm these reserved but witty people.

A host of Estonian sayings confirms this thrifty approach to words: "First think, then say it"; "Weigh everything carefully seven times before making a move"; "Talking is silver, silence is gold"; and the rather chilling "May thy face be as ice". Estonians like their personal space: Russian bear hugs are not for them (unless you know them very well). Traditionally, a neighbour's house is quite close enough, thank you, if you can see the smoke

▶ Silence is golden

"People coming from the south note the pauses that Estonians do not hurry to fill with words. Silence is a friend, not an enemy. If you come to Estonia by car or bus, you won't see mountains. The road is lined with trees, kilometres and kilometres of forest. It is from such a landscape, amid the stillness, that Estonians come. Although a lot of forest has been cleared and most people have moved to the towns, Estonians would still rather seek out nature than go to church. They go to listen to the silence, just like their ancestors, who, before the arrival of the Knights of the Sword, used to go to a scarred heath to converse with their gods."

Triin Sinissaar, playwright (one of Estonia's few contemporary female playwrights).

from the chimney. Ask an Estonian where the best beach is and he or she will direct you to the least crowded one, preferably one you can have all to yourself. Estonians like forests and empty landscapes; like the mobile phones they are so fond of, they need regular peace and quiet to recharge. When they complain that a remote island has become too crowded, they are probably referring to the occasional party of Finnish cyclists, not a horde of tourists.

Estonians are quietly romantic, but they are not prone to fits of passion, especially in public. When the jilted lover of an Italian restaurant-owner in Tallinn had the faithless man murdered, Estonians were relieved to learn that the vengeful woman was Russian. In Jaan Kross's short story *The Ashtray*, an Estonian political prisoner in transit in Russia strikes up a conversation with a detainee from Romania and reflects: "I have always had difficulties in reacting to a southern temperament. The likes of us – or at least of myself – do not understand it entirely. One never knows how thick the space is between outer shell and core. Where theatricality ends and gravity begins. Is everything merely stage-setting, or does it all come straight from the heart?"

Estonians are also pragmatic. Cast as a 'subject people' by various invaders, they are used to getting around officialdom and the silly restraints imposed on them. Being stubborn is seen as a virtue. They do not like being told what to do, even when they want to do what they are being told to do, such as vote 'yes' in the referendum on joining the European Union. They are deeply libertarian and really don't care what people get up to, so long as it doesn't affect them. They are impressed not by status, but by what you have achieved. Estonian folk tales are not about knights, nobles or kings; instead, their heroes are down-to-earth, clever people who trick the boss or double-cross invaders.

When you talk to Estonians, the trick is not to confuse reticence and a lack of pretension with being cold-hearted, dull or miserable. They party (and drink) as hard as they work. They have a good sense of humour and make loyal and generous friends. They are unsnobbish and discreet, and they respect your personal space. Suffering the silence is worth it in the end.

Index

Credits

Footprint credits

Text editor: Sophie Blacksell
Map editor: Sarah Sorensen
Picture editor: Robert Lunn
Publisher: Patrick Dawson
Editorial: Angus Dawson, Nicola Jones,
Felicity Laughton, Alan Murphy
Cartography: Claire Benison, Kevin
Feeney, Robert Lunn,
Sarah Sorensen.
Sales and Marketing: Andy Riddle
Advertising: Debbie Wylde
Administration: Elizabeth Taylor
Series development: Rachel Fielding
Design: Mytton Williams

Photography credits

Front cover: Alamy
Inside: H. Laan, T. Tuul (Lahemaa,
p103)
Generic images: John Matchett
Back cover: Tallinn Tourist Office

Print

Manufactured in India by Nutech
Photolithographers
Pulp from sustainable forests

® Footprint Handbooks and the
Footprint mark are a registered
trademark of Footprint Handbooks Ltd

Every effort has been made to ensure
that the facts in this guide are accurate.
However the authors and publishers
cannot accept responsibility for any loss,
injury or inconvenience sustained by
any traveller as a result of information or
advice contained in this guide.

Publishing information

Footprint 2006
2nd edition
Text and maps © Footprint Handbooks
Ltd July 2006

ISBN 1 904777 77 5
CIP DATA: a catalogue record for this
book is available from the British
Library

Published by Footprint
6 Riverside Court
Lower Bristol Road
Bath BA2 3DZ, UK
T+44 (0)1225 469141
F+44 (0)1225 469461
discover@footprintbooks.com
www.footprintbooks.com

Distributed in the USA by Publishers
Group West

Publishing stuff

Complete title list

Siena & the heart of Tuscany (P)
Spain
Tallinn (P)
Turin (P)
Turkey
Valencia (P)
Verona (P)
Wales

Latin America & Caribbean

Antigua & Leeward
  Islands (P)
Argentina
Barbados (P)
Bolivia
Brazil
Caribbean Islands
Central America & Mexico
Chile
Colombia
Costa Rica
Cuba
Cusco & the Inca Trail
Dominican Republic (P)
Ecuador & Galápagos
Havana (P)
Mexico
Nicaragua
Peru
Rio de Janeiro (P)
South American Handbook
St Lucia (P)
Venezuela

Middle East

Dubai (P)
Jordan
Syria & Lebanon

North America

New York (P)
Vancouver (P)
Western Canada

Discover guides

Belize, Guatemala & Southern Mexico
East Coast Australia
Patagonia
Peru, Bolivia & Ecuador
Vietnam, Cambodia & Laos
Western Canada

Lifestyle guides

Diving the World
European City Breaks
Surfing Britain
Surfing Europe
Surfing the World

(P) denotes pocket guide

Publishing stuff

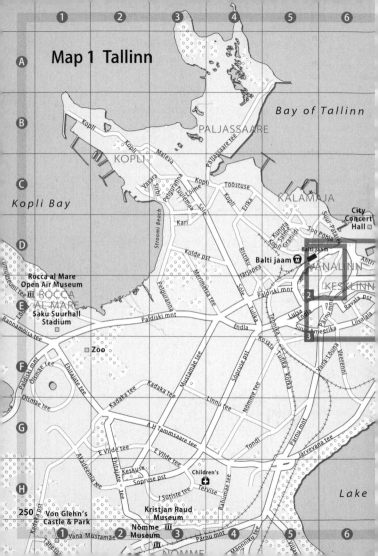

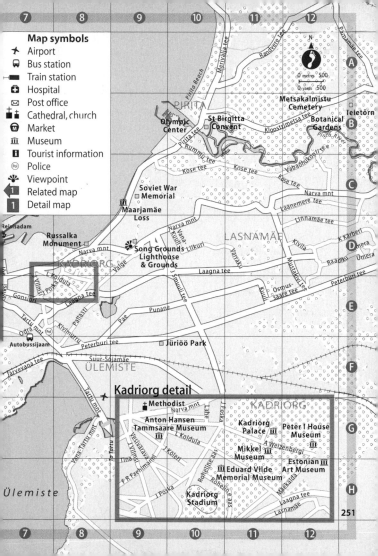

Map symbols

✈ Airport
🚌 Bus station
🚆 Train station
➕ Hospital
✉ Post office
⛪ Cathedral, church
🎭 Market
🏛 Museum
ℹ Tourist information
ⓟ Police
☀ Viewpoint
1 Related map
1 Detail map

PIRITA

St Birgitta Convent

Olympic Center

Metsakalmistu Cemetery

Botanical Gardens

Teletõrn

Metsavalla tee

Randvere tee

Pärnamäe tee

Pirita Beach

Kloostrimetsa tee

Pirita River

Vabaõhukooli tee

Pirita tee

Rummu tee

Kose tee

Kose tee

Soviet War Memorial

Maarjamäe Loss

Narva mnt

Vana-Kuuli

Liikuri

Laanemere tee

Linnamäe tee

LASNAMÄE

K Karberi

Õmera

Õmera

Raadiku

Reisisadam

Russalka Monument

Narva mnt

KADRIORG

L Koidula

Vilmsi Poska

Gonsiori

Laagna tee

Song Grounds Lighthouse & Grounds

Valge

Laagna tee

Vana-Kuuli

Varraku

Kuuli

Mustakivi tee

Osmussaare tee

Peterburi tee

Tartu mnt

Odra mnt

Kivimurru

Pallasti

Pae

Punane

Peterburi tee

Jüriöö Park

Autobussijaam

Suur-Sõjamäe

Järvevana tee

ÜLEMISTE

Ülemiste

Vana-Tartu mnt

Tartu mnt

Tp Tartu

Kadriorg detail

KADRIORG

✝ Methodist

Narva mnt

Anton Hansen Tammsaare Museum

L Koidula

Kadriorg Palace

Mikkel Museum

Peter I House Museum

Estonian Art Museum

Eduard Vilde Memorial Museum

Kadriorg Stadium

Lille

J Poska

A Weizenbergi

Roheline aas

Roheline aas

Vesivärava

J Köleri

F R Faehlmanni

J Poska

Tiina

Mäekalda

Laagna tee

Lasnamäe

251

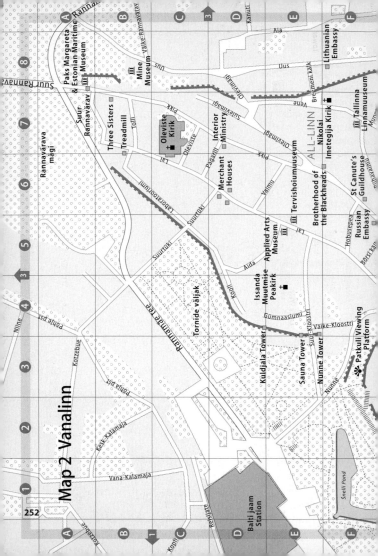

Map 2 Vanalinn

Paks Margareta & Estonian Maritime Museum

Suur Rannavärav

Rannavärava mägi

Three Sisters

Treadmill

Mine Museum

Oleviste Kirik

Merchant Houses

Interior Ministry

Tervishoiumuuseum

Applied Arts Museum

Issanda Muutmise Peakirik

Tornide väljak

Kuldjala Tower

Sauna Tower

Nunne Tower

Brotherhood of the Blackheads

ALL-LINN

Nikolai

Imetegija Kirik

St Canute's Guildhouse

Hobusepea Russian Embassy

Patkuli Viewing Platform

Lithuanian Embassy

Tallinna Linnamuuseum

Balti jaam Station

Snelli Pond

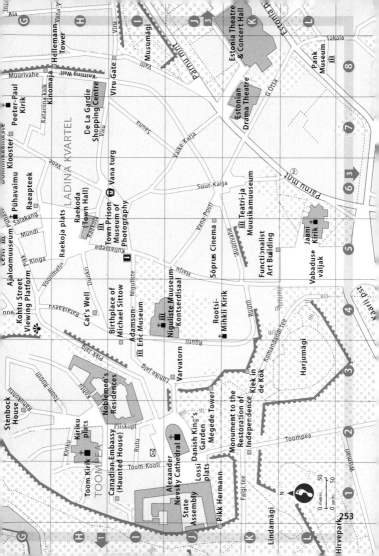

G · H · I · J · K · L

3 Estonia Theatre & Concert Hall

Aia

Viru

Müürivahe

Knitting Wall

Hellemann/Vana-v Tower

Peeter-Paul Kirik

Katariina käik

Kinomaja

Pühavaimu

Raeapteek

De La Gardie Shopping Centre

Viru Gate

Viru

Sauna

Väike-Karja

Musumägi

Pärnu mnt

Vaili

Estonian Drama Theatre

G Otsa

Pank Museum

Sakala

8

Dominikaanese Klooster

LADINA KVARTEL

Vene

Pikk

Salakäng

Mündi

Lai

Ajaloomuuseum

Voorimehe

Kohtu Street Viewing Platform

Pikk

Kinga

Dunkri

Rataskaevu

Cat's Well

Raekoja plats

Raekoda (Town Hall)

Raekägu

Kullassepa

Town Prison Museum of Photography

Vana turg

Suur-Karja

Vana-Posti

Teatri-ja Muusikamuuseum

Müürivahe

Sõprus Cinema

Functionalist Art Building

Jaani Kirik

7

6 3

Pärnu mnt **2**

Vabaduse väljak

5

Estonia pst

4

Birthplace of Michael Sittow

Adamson-Eric Museum

Niguliste

Niguliste Muuseum-Kontserdisaal

Rootsi-Mihkli Kirik

Rüütli

Lühike jalg

Varvatorn

Kiriku

Pikk jalg

Toom-Rüütli

Stenbock House

Rahukohtu

Noblemen's Residences

Kohtu

Pikk jalg

Kiriku plats

Piiskopi

Megede Tower

Ruutli

Komandandi tee

Harjumägi

Monument to the Restoration of Independence

Kiek in de Kök

3 2

Kiriku

Toom Kirik

TOOMPEA

Canadian Embassy (Haunted House)

Rutu

Alexander Nevsky Cathedral

Danish King's Garden

Toompea

Toom-Kooli

Lossi plats

Komandandi tee

Falgi tee

Wismari

Wismari

1

State Assembly

Pikk Hermann

Lindamägi

Hirvepark

N

0 metres 50

0 yards 50

253

G · H · I · J · K · L

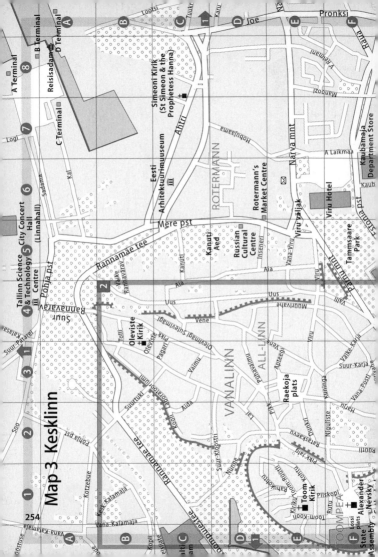

Map 3 Kesklinn

A Terminal
B Terminal
D Terminal
Reisisadam
C Terminal

Logi

Loots

Tuuli

Karu

Joe

Pronksi

Hbuild

**Simeoni Kirik
(St Simeon & the
Prophetess Hanna)**

Ahtri

**Eesti
Arhitektuurimuuseum**

Hobujaama

ROTERMANN

Narva mnt

A Laikmaa

Kaubamaja

**Kaubamaja
Department Store**

Kaub

Viru väljak

**Rotermann's
Market Centre**

Viru Hotel

**City Concert
Hall
(Linnahall)**

Sadama

Kalaranna

Kalasadama

Mere pst

Rannamäe tee

Suur Rannavärav

Pohja pst

Kotzebue

Vana-Kalamaja

Kesk-Kalamaja

Soo

Suur-Patarei

**Tallinn Science
& Technology
Centre**

Vaike Rannavärav

Kanuti

Toll

Oleviste

**Oleviste
Kirik**

Pagari

Uus

Vene

Uus

Väimu

Aida

Olevimägi Sulevimägi

Pikk Sulevimägi

Lai

Suur-Kloostri

Aida

Vaimu

**Kanuti
Aed**

**Russian
Cultural
Centre**

Inseneri

Aia

Vana-Viru

Viru-Viru

Vana-Viru

Viru

VANALINN

ALL-LINN

Vene

Maaivahe

Vaimu

Apteegi

Pühavaimu

Niguliste

Kuninga

Harju

Rüütli

Dunkri

Ratskaevu

Raekoja

**Raekoja
plats**

Mündi

Viru

Valli

Pärnu mnt

**Tammsaare
Park**

Pärnu mnt

Tartu mnt

Valli

Vana-Posti

Suur-Karja

Valke-Karja

Suur-Karja

Pikk Jalg

Kohtu

Toom-Rüütli

Toom-Kooli

**Toom
Kirik**

Kloostri

Piiskopi

Toom-Kooli

Rahukohtu

TOOMPEA

Lossi plats

**State
Assembly**

**Alexander
Nevsky**

Kaarmann

Veerenni

Manezi

Kiratori

Vilmsi

Kunderi

Karu

Rannamäe tee

Toompuiestee

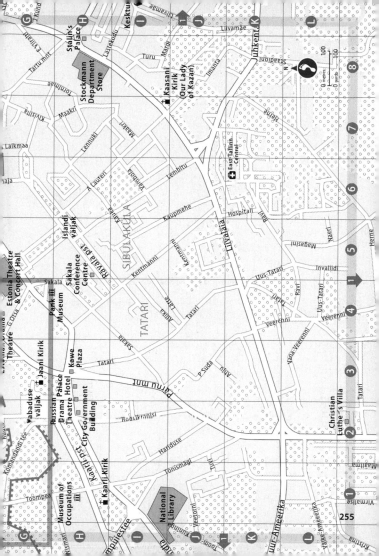

Map 4 Around Tallinn

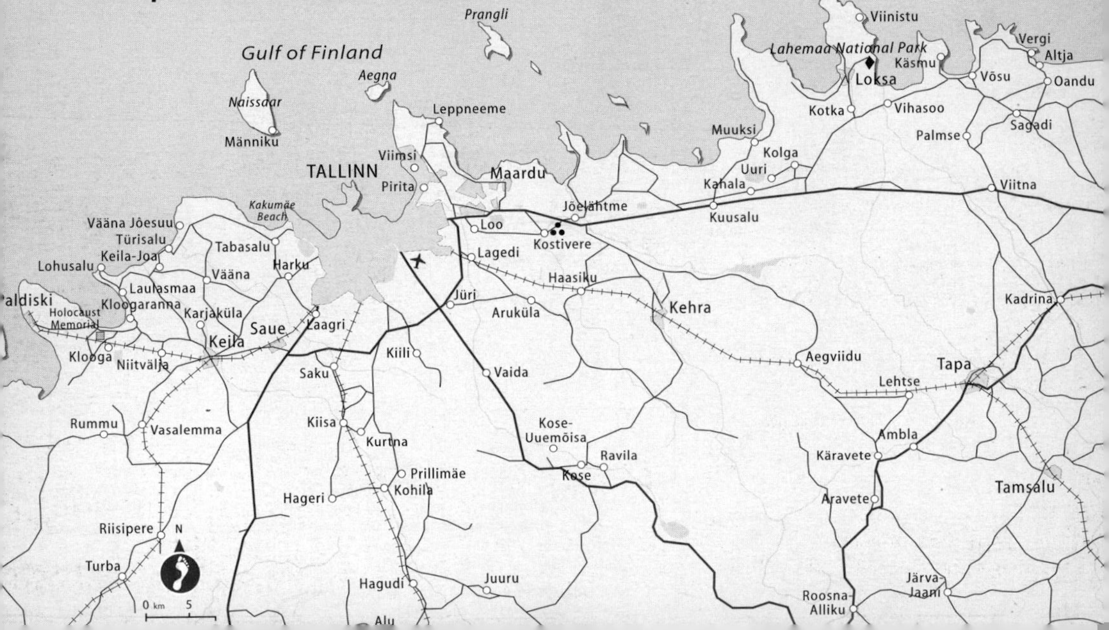

Gulf of Finland

Prangli

Aegna

Naissaar

Männiku

TALLINN

Pirita

Viimsi

Leppneeme

Maardu

Lahemaa National Park

Vergi
Altja
Oandu
Vösu
Sagadi
Viinistu
Käsmu
Loksa
Palmse
Vihasoo
Kotka
Kotka
Kolga
Uuri
Muuksi
Kahala
Kuusalu

Viitna
Kadrina
Tapa
Tamsalu
Lehtse
Ambla
Aegviidu
Käravete
Aravete
Järva-Jaani
Roosna-Alliku

Kehra

Jõelähtme
Kostivere
Loo
Lagedi
Jüri
Haasiku
Aruküla
Vaida
Kose-Uuemõisa
Kose
Ravila
Juuru

Kiili
Kurtna
Prillimäe
Kohila
Hagudi
Alu

Laagri
Saku
Kiisa
Hageri

Harku
Tabasalu
Väana
Saue
Keila
Karjaküla

Kokumäe Beach

Väana-Jõesuu
Turisalu
Keila-Joa
Lohusalu
Laulasmaa
Kloogarand
Klooga
Niitväla
Rummu
Vasalemma
Riisipere
Turba

Holocaust Memorial

aldiski

0 km 5

N